GREEK TRAGEDY AND THE EMOTIONS

An introductory study

W. B. Stanford

Routledge & Kegan Paul
London, Boston, Melbourne and Henley

First published in 1983
by Routledge & Kegan Paul plc
39 Store Street, London WC1E 7DD,
9 Park Street, Boston, Mass. 02108, USA,
464 St Kilda Road, Melbourne,
Victoria 3004, Australia, and
Broadway House, Newtown Road,
Henley-on-Thames, Oxon RG9 1EN
Photoset in 11 on 13 Garamond by
Kelly Typesetting Ltd, Bradford-on-Avon, Wiltshire
and printed in Great Britain by
The Thetford Press Ltd, Thetford, Norfolk
© W. B. Stanford 1983

Library of Congress Cataloging in Publication Data

Stanford, William Bedell.

Greek tragedy and the emotions : *etc*
Bibliography: p.
Includes index.
1. Greek drama (Tragedy) – History and criticism.
I. Title
PA3131.S78   1983   882'.01'09   83–8676

ISBN 0–7100–9554–6

Contents

Preface

My grateful thanks are due to many for advice and encouragement in composing this rather recalcitrant book. Above all to Professor A. A. Long, Mr A. E. Hinds and my wife (as always) who read all through various drafts and suggested valuable improvements. And then, in matters of detail, to Professor John Boardman, Mr Godfrey W. Bond, Mr Robert Boerum and Professor T. M. Falkner of Wooster College, Ohio (where the final chapters were written in a very congenial environment), Sir Kenneth Dover, Professor D. W. Forrest, Professor T. N. Mitchell, Dr L. E. R. Picken, Professor Charles Segal, Dr Oliver Taplin, my son-in-law Michael O'Regan, and my son Philip – as well as to many other colleagues and friends who tolerantly endured conversations about it. None of these is responsible for any lapses in the final version as now presented. It might have been better to follow Horace's advice and let the book mature in cask, so to speak, for nine years. But *ars longa*, *vita brevis*, especially when an author has passed his seventy-second year.

At any rate, I hope that what I offer may help to stimulate further and better work on this rather neglected, but as I believe, important, aspect of Greek tragedy.

Trinity College, Dublin   W. B. Stanford

CHAPTER ONE

The centrality of emotionalism

Q. What was the aim of the dramatists of the classical period in Athens?

A. To win a prize at the Dionysian festival.

Q. How did they do that?

A. By being best at giving their audiences the pleasure of laughing and crying.

Q. How did the tragedians make their audiences cry?

A. That would take a whole book to answer.

Q. Can you recommend one?

A. I don't know of any.

Q. Why on earth isn't there, if, as you say, emotions were so important in Greek tragedy?

A. I can't say for certain. Perhaps because emotions are so subjective and so hard to define. Or perhaps because scholars prefer to discuss what goes on in the mind rather than what involves the heart. Or perhaps because the spectre of 'the affective fallacy' warns them off.

Q. Well, shouldn't there be one?

A. Yes, I certainly think so.

Q. Why don't you write one?

A. I'll try, if you really think one is needed.

That was more or less the dialectic, conducted with several helpful scholars, that led to the present book. In view of the emphasis given by the ancient critics to the emotional elements in Greek tragedy, it is surprising that there is no comprehensive book on the subject. Much indeed has been written about the tragic emotions, in the light (or darkness) of Aristotle's theory of catharsis. But these studies have mostly been concerned

1

about how to reduce or get rid of the emotions roused by Greek tragedy and not about how they were stimulated and sustained. As a further result of Aristotle's influence such discussions have generally been confined to the Great Twin Brethren of the Catharsis, pity and fear. But the gamut of emotions played on by the tragedians was far wider than that.

The strangest phenomenon of all is that many of the most able and influential writers and commentators on Greek tragedy in modern times have ignored its emotional elements almost entirely. You may search through their publications without finding more than cursory references to pity, fear, anger, grief, hate, scorn, or any of the other tragic emotions, and often there is no reference to them at all. Yet, if we are to believe the ancient critics, the essence of tragedy is in the emotions that it expressed and caused. There have been a few exceptions to this neglect of tragic emotionalism, beginning with Nietzsche's much maligned and much misrepresented *Birth of Tragedy* in 1872. Since then a small number of relevant books, essays and dissertations have been published, as listed in my bibliography. I am much indebted to several of these, as well as to the scattered remarks of those editors who have recognized the importance of emotionalism in Greek tragedy. But all of them are restricted to particular aspects of the subject, and they are mostly concerned with considering how the tragedians *described* emotions and have little or nothing to say about how they *aroused* them in the audiences. What is ultimately needed is a book on tragic *páthos* (in the wider Greek sense of that term) to match Wilhelm Suess's work on the other dominant element in Greek literature, *êthos*, the portrayal and expression of character (which Aristotle ranked below *páthos* in his *Poetics*). The present work has no pretensions to equalling the scope and depth of that masterly study. As my title-page indicates, it is only an introductory study. But I hope that it may help towards a definitive book in the future.

The subject of the present work, then, is how the Athenian tragedians made their characters and choruses cry with pity, shudder with fear, storm with rage, strain with suspense, dance with joy and spit with hate, and how these representations of emotionalism affected their audiences – an emotionalism that is rarely if ever paralleled in modern performances of tragedy. We laugh freely and openly at comedies, but we seldom cry or tremble at tragedies, except in the cinema for reasons to be considered later. (Theodoros, the celebrated actor of fifth-century Athens, remarked that there was nothing wonderful about making people laugh: the wonderful thing was to make them cry, Plutarch, *Moralia* 545F.) The low temperature of emotionalism in our theatres is partly due, no doubt, to the cooler temperaments of northern latitudes, and also to the cult of 'the stiff upper lip' that evolved in Britain during the nineteenth century. But basic differences in the nature and setting of ancient and modern tragedy, as will be described later, must also be considered. If one seeks a contemporary equivalent to the emotional excitement of the Athenian theatre one will find it at 'rock' concerts or football matches. They retain emotive elements that our theatres have lost.

The evidence for this strong emotionalism among Greek theatrical audiences comes partly from literary critics and partly from historians. In the first half of the fourth century BC Plato, all the better as a witness for being hostile, in his *Republic* (605C-D) deplored tragedy's 'utterly alarming' emotional power. 'Even the best of us', he testified, 'when we listen to a passage from Homer or from a tragedy in which a grieving hero is represented as dragging out his sorrows in a long speech and people sing and beat their breasts – then, as you know, we delight in surrendering ourselves . . .', to which Socrates' interlocutor replies, 'Indeed I know that: how could it be otherwise?' In a later passage, warranted to distress Freudians, Socrates deplores the fact that tragedy 'rouses and feeds and waters' the passions instead of 'drying them up': it lets them take control of the *psuché*, usurping the control of the mind. In *Laws* 800D the Athenian speaker in the dialogue deprecates the fact that prizes are won by the choruses that are best at 'straining' the *psuché* of audiences 'with words and

3

rhythms and mournful tunes' and at making them cry (cf. Aeschines 3, 153). In *Philebos* 48A Socrates considers the paradox that people enjoy surrendering themselves to grief. (Ambiguities in the word *psuché* will be described in chapter 7.)

Plato's moralistic and utilitarian attitude to poetry is often attributed also to Aristophanes because in his *Frogs* he presented Aeschylus and Euripides as attacking and defending each other's tragedies on the basis of their didactic value. But, apart from the possibility that this may be a caricature of contemporary utilitarianism, in the end Dionysos makes his decision in favour of Aeschylus on the grounds that he gives him more pleasure, and 'I shall choose the one whom my *psuché* desires' (1413, 1468; cf. 916, 1028). This emotional and hedonistic attitude to tragedy on the part of the god of the theatre may well reflect the view of the average Athenian and, indeed of Aristophanes himself. It was certainly the view of many subsequent literary critics of good repute.

Aristotle in his defence of tragedy in his *Poetics* did not deny Plato's allegations about its emotional power. Nor did he, as one might have expected from so rational a critic, minimize the irrational element. Instead, as every student of literary theory knows, he insisted that 'the proper pleasure' of tragedy was achieved 'by means of pity, and fear, and suchlike emotions' (*Poetics* 1449b 27–8). In his theory of catharsis he was to some extent following the doctrine of Gorgias who in his encomium of Helen (8–9) emphasized the power of the spoken word, especially poetry, to arouse and assuage terror, pity and yearning. In general the power of oratory to move audiences by emotive methods was widely recognized in antiquity. In fact, several rhetoricians considered it the orator's chief weapon in the art of persuasion. Oratory was highly histrionic, just as parts of tragedy were highly rhetorical. In what follows here, classical views on the *páthos* of oratory and of tragedy will be regarded as interchangeable, with some reservations.

Literary critics after Aristotle continued to describe and emphasize the emotive elements in drama and oratory. The author of the treatise commonly known as *On the Sublime* wrote a monograph on *páthos*, but it is lost. The term used by him and by other writers for the power of arousing and controlling the emotions was *psuchagōgía*, literally 'leading the *psuchē*'. The historian Polybios contrasted (2, 56, 11) tragedy's ability to overwhelm the feelings and 'lead the *psuchē*' with the more rational functions of history. The Stoic philosophers with their doctrine of *apátheia* supported Plato in his hostility to this emotionalism, and some Christian apologists followed them. Tertullian in his general denunciation of the public spectacles condemned tragedy's arousal of anger, grief, frenzy and similar violent emotions, which affected even moderate and respectable members of the audience (*De Spectaculis* 15). He consoled those who were sorry to be deprived of such scenes by promising them that from heaven they would observe even greater lamentations and agonies among the damned in Hell (*De Spectaculis* 30). St Augustine in his unredeemed youth enjoyed weeping in the theatre, but later he deplored such pleasure as 'a shameful itch' (*turpis scabies*, *Confessions* 3, 2).

The earliest historian to mention the emotional power of tragedy was Herodotos. In a well-known passage (6, 21) he records that when Phrynichos in 494 BC produced his tragedy on the recent capture and sack of Miletos by the Persians the Athenian audience 'fell into weeping' so distressingly that the magistrates fined the dramatist heavily and banned further performances of the play. Herodotos' reference is brief, but he implies an outburst of mass hysteria that threatened law and order. The primary cause of this extreme grief was, no doubt, the recent disaster to a city closely linked racially and sentimentally with Athens. But the emotion was presumably enhanced by the dramatic art of the playwright. It was a different matter when, nearly ninety years later, an audience, shortly after the death of Euripides, burst into tears at the sight of Sophocles and his chorus entering the theatre dressed as mourners (*Life of Euripides* 2, 11, Schwartz). That was not part of the drama.

The next historical testimony comes from Xenophon in his *Symposium* (3, 11). He states that the tragic actor Callipides prided himself on being able 'to fill the seats with weeping multitudes'. A wave of fear is attested by a much later witness, Plutarch, who records (*Moralia* 998E) that at a performance of a lost play by Euripides an audience rose to its feet in terror when a mother was about to kill her son in ignorance. It may have been the same play, *Cresphontes*, or else *Trojan Women*, that melted the heart of the tyrant Alexander of Pherai as described by Plutarch in his life of Pelopidas (29, cf. Aelian, *Varia Historia* 14, 40): he burst into tears at a pitiful scene and rushed out of the theatre, confessing later that he was ashamed to have been moved more by a theatrical show than by the sufferings of his own subjects (cf. Isocrates 4, 168).

These are examples of sympathetic feeling. A notorious instance of personal and subjective emotion on the part of an audience is recorded in the anonymous *Life of Aeschylus*. It states that at the beginning of his *Eumenides* the spectators were so shocked by the frightful appearance of the Furies that children fainted and women had miscarriages – an incident hardly to be paralleled in the history of the theatre. Its authenticity has been challenged, but the record of some such strong emotional reaction may be true, since Aeschylus was notoriously expert in theatrical shock-tactics. (It is generally assumed that the terror was caused entirely by the visual appearance of the Furies, but that view will be questioned on a later page.)

Much of the emotional effectiveness of classical drama seems to have resulted from the music and dancing as Nietzsche emphasized. Lucian in his essay on the dance (83) cites an incident when a performer danced the madness of Ajax – perhaps from Sophocles' play, but more likely a later solo part – so well that the whole theatre went mad with him, jumping and shouting and throwing their clothes in the air. Dion of Prusa in his discourse to the Alexandrians (32, 55–6) rebuked the audiences of that rather hysterical city for their outrageous conduct at similar performances: 'You sit dumbfounded or

6

you leap about more violently than the dancers themselves; you get all tensed up like people in a drunken frenzy . . . or like barbarians after inhaling some kind of drug.' Things were worse, Dion complains (32, 74), among the spectators in the stadium, with shouts, uproar, bodily contortions, cursing, jumping about, raving, people beating and abusing one another, reviling the gods, throwing away their belongings, sometimes stripping themselves naked. Dion sadly observes that while Orpheus tamed wild beasts by his music, here in Alexandria performing musicians turn human beings into savages.

These last descriptions are not about the theatre in classical Athens, and one must not imagine that such extremes of conduct – similar to those in our crowds at football matches or 'rock' concerts – were frequent there. But on the other hand the Athenian audiences were probably closer to them than to our staid theatregoers. Plato complains in his *Republic* (492B) that when they assembled *en masse* in the theatre or law-courts or political gatherings they customarily made such a din that the surrounding places re-echoed their noises (cf. Aristophanes, *Ecclesiazousai* 395–430). Sometimes the sudden reactions of Athenian audiences were provoked by moral indignation (*némesis*, to be discussed in chapter 3) rather than by grief or fear. Seneca (Letters 115, 15) records that when a character in Euripides' last play *Danaë* praised gold as the finest thing for mortals, giving more pleasure than one's mother or children or dear father, the whole audience stood up in protest at the unworthy sentiment. And on another occasion, Euripides with his fondness for making his characters say outrageous things got into similar trouble: when that sturdy moralist Antisthenes the proto-Cynic heard the line in *Aiolos*

What's shameful if the users think it not so?

he shouted back in a matching iambic trimeter,

Shameful is shame whether it seems so or not
(Plutarch, *Moralia* 33C).

7

For a similar reason Socrates walked out of the theatre in disapproval of a line in Euripides' *Auge* which asked that virtue should be let 'roam at will'. But on the other hand he was so pleased at the opening lines of *Orestes* with their assertion of the power of human endurance that he called for an encore (Cicero, *Tusculan Disputations* 4, 29, 63). If Euripides was encouraged by this good beginning he must have been all the more deeply chagrined when later in that play an actor mispronounced a line with such a ludicrous accentuation that the audience broke into peals of laughter, as will be noticed later.

Athenian audiences still express their feelings noisily and forcefully at times. During the centenary celebrations of the University of Athens in 1937, when the dictatorship of Metaxas was at its height, *Antigone* was performed before foreign delegates and local dignitaries in the Theatre of Herodes Atticus. As soon as Teiresias spoke the line (1056)

The breed of tyrants ever loves base gain,

Athenians in the audience joyfully cheered and applauded for some minutes. It was a brave gesture since people were being imprisoned for much less. But unlike the incidents described earlier, it had probably been planned in advance.

To turn from audiences to authors and actors: Aristotle asserts (*Poetics* 1455a 31–2) that if a poet wants to make others feel the storms of emotion he must first feel them himself. Horace confirms this in his celebrated maxim (*Ars Poetica* 102 ff.), 'If you want to make me cry, you must feel the grief yourself.' Similarly a character in Euripides' *Suppliant Women* (180–3) asserts that if a poet wants to give joy to his audience, he must feel joy himself. Quintilian (6, 2, 34) recommends this kind of empathy for orators, and so, too, Cicero in his *De Oratore* (2, 45, 189, and 46, 193). Quintilian speaking of actors says that he has often seen them in tears after an emotional scene. There is no description in classical Greek literature of similar personal emotionalism on the part of actors. But we have Plato's celebrated account in *Ion* 535C of a rhapsode

8

reciting epic poetry – how his eyes fill with tears, his pulse beats faster and even his hair stands on end.

Modern testimony to bardic emotionalism is to be found in an unpublished journal by a traveller in Greece in 1749. He visited the monastery of Kaisariani on the western slopes of Hymettos. The Abbot recited a passage from Homer: 'He seemed in Exstasy – totally enraptured – his Eyes rolled – His features were chang'd and in every Particular he appear'd like Virgil's Sibyl "full of the God".' Similarly Plutarch in his life of Demosthenes (9, 4) records that the orator often became 'like a Bacchanal' (*parábakchos*) in his speeches. It is not unlikely that at climactic moments in tragedy actors and choruses would behave with similar emotionalism.

Plato, in the passage just quoted from his *Ion*, adds that this *enthousiasmós* of the rhapsode infected the audience in the same way as a magnet magnetizes metal objects. Dionysios of Halicarnassos (*Demosthenes* 22) says that he did not need any speaker to give him a similar effect. He could feel it even when he read a speech of Demosthenes – reading it aloud, of course – for himself:

> But whenever I take up any of the speeches of
> Demosthenes I get possessed with a kind of ecstasy
> (*enthousiô*) and I am led this way and that, changing one
> emotion for another, doubt, agony, fear, scorn, hate,
> pity, benevolence, anger, spite, taking in turn all the
> emotions that have the natural power to master the human
> mind. And it seems to me that there is no difference
> between me in this condition and the people who are being
> initiated into the rites of the Great Mother and the
> Corybantes and other rites of that kind.

Dionysios goes on to say that when the written words of Demosthenes had such an effect, their power to move those who actually heard him speak them must have been astounding. Aristotle, as one would expect from a less exuberant critic, confirms this in a quieter way. Twice (*Poetics* 1450b 18–19, 1462a 11–13) he assures us that tragedy's 'proper pleasure', that

9

is, the arousal and catharsis of emotions, can be experienced 'without performance'.

But naturally, as Dionysios understood, actual perform-ances would enhance the emotionalism. Occasionally, it seems, actors used adventitious aids to heighten it. According to Aulus Gellius (*Attic Nights* 6, 5) when the fourth-century actor Polos was playing the part of Electra in the scene of Sophocles' play in which she receives the urn supposed to contain the ashes of her brother, he substituted the funerary urn of his own recently dead son, giving special poignancy to the lines (1120–2),

> . . . Oh let me take it in my hands
> That I may weep and have my fill of woe
> Both for myself and all my race as well.

One hopes, however, that the audience were unaware of the substitution. Otherwise they would have felt cross-currents of pity for Electra and for Polos that would have disturbed the flow of the play.

All this emotionalism is far from the great Delphic maxim, 'Do nothing excessively', a maxim that is frequently pro-claimed in Greek tragedy. But it is a moral maxim, not an artistic one, except in terms of style and structure. Tragedy thrives on excess. The greatest of the Greek tragedies centre on acts of extreme suffering and their consequences – brutal deaths and suicides, agonizing pain, incest, rape, human sacrifice, cannibalism, mutilations, screams of pain, floods of tears, spoutings of blood, as will be discussed in later chapters. The paradox, which lies at the heart of all true tragedy, is that by the magic of the word, as Gorgias called it, these terrible and pitiful deeds ultimately give pleasure by the drama's *psuchagōgía*. Racine spoke for the Greek tragedians as well as for himself when he affirmed in the preface to *Bérénice*, 'La principale règle est de plaire et de toucher: toutes les autres ne sont faites que pour parvenir à cette première.' And, as Nietzsche so clearly saw, in essence Greek tragedy was Dionysian not Apollonian.

CHAPTER TWO

The conditions of performance

Three main factors contribute to emotionalism in a theatre – the temperaments and moods of the audiences, the physical and psychological conditions of the performances, and the nature of the plays being performed. Evidence for the excitability of the ancient Athenians has already been presented. The emotive elements in the tragedies themselves will be considered later. This chapter is concerned with the setting of the dramas, which was so different in many ways from that of a modern theatre. The facts offered will be familiar to all well-informed students of Greek drama, but the interpretations may be less familiar and perhaps more controversial.

Our modern theatrical performances are generally presented in a place devoted to secular entertainment, though there have been exceptions like T. S. Eliot's *Murder in the Cathedral*. In contrast, the performances at the City Dionysia, where most of the tragedies were presented, were part of a religious celebration in the sacred precinct of Dionysos with his high priest enthroned in the centre of the front row. The performances were preceded by sacrifices and libations, while an altar (the *thumélē*) stood in the centre of the orchestra. As a result, the initial mood of the audiences would have resembled that of a modern congregation at a festival liturgy rather than that of theatre-goers in our time. Indeed the liturgy of the Eastern Orthodox Church with its solemn entrances and processions, its rich robes and pageantry, its speeches and dialogues, its symbolical gestures and emotional climaxes, its singing and chanting, its alternations of grief and joy, has much in common with the pagan tragic performances. Both ceremonies share the name and nature of a 'liturgy', *leitourgía*, 'a public service'. In

11

the early Christian era bishops and emperors, being aware of
the seductive emotionalism of the traditional theatre, banned
it, as Plato had recommended, though they allowed the cruder
excitements of the amphitheatre and hippodrome to continue.
Julian the Apostate in one of his letters (7.222A) pleaded the
beneficial effects of the Dionysiac cult, arguing that anyone
who had not experienced its ritual frenzy was in danger of
psychological disintegration, as Pentheus was physically torn
asunder for his resistance to Dionysos. But it was in vain. Soon
the theatres of Bacchos were finally closed in favour of
churches dedicated to Holy Wisdom and Holy Peace, and the
ōmophagía of the old religion became the Holy Eucharist of the
new. Yet one echo of the ancient cult survived. The literary
drama called *The Passion of Christ*, attributed to Gregory of
Nazianzus, used many phrases and lines from *Bacchai* to describe the agony of Christ and the sorrow of his Mother – a
strange blending of Christian and pagan emotionalism. It is still
dramatically harrowing, as recent performances by a Greek
company proved.

One of the greatest triumphs of the Athenians' talent for
civilizing the raw materials of life and nature came in the sixth
and early fifth centuries BC when they transformed the savage
Dionysiac cult into a superb art form. In its primitive period it
embodied the frenzied dances and the wild cries of the ecstatic
votaries, the ritual rending asunder of live animals, and the
eating of their raw, blood-dripping flesh. Then came the controlled dances and songs of the dithyrambic choruses organized on a tribal basis in Athens. Finally these evolved into the
full tragedies of the classical period, and then, as Aristotle
affirms in his *Poetics* (1449a 15), tragedy having reached its full
stature stopped growing.

So the evolution was from 'orgy' in the Greek sense of that
word – that is, high excitement and emotionalism in a crowd or
group – through tribal dances (in which the dancers were
surrogates for the whole community) to disciplined drama.
But was the orgiastic spirit of the original cult entirely extinct
among fifth-century Athenian audiences? We know on good

fourth-century evidence (Plato, *Laws* 775B, and Philochoros cited in Athenaios 464F) that during the Dionysian festival the Athenians customarily drank wine before the theatrical performances. This, as Plutarch (*Moralia* 656C) says, stimulated their imagination while it confused their intellects. As they came crowding into the theatre they would see the temple and the emblems of the god who had the power to drive people temporarily out of their senses. Did they then feel a certain *frisson* of pleasurable fear as they entered the precinct, such as modern visitors might feel when approaching a site associated with witchcraft or diabolism? When the play began and they heard the music of the pipe and the beat of the dancers' feet, and watched the choruses weave in and out in their complex patterns, did they, irrespective of the verbal content of the dramas, experience vestiges of the ecstatic delirium that the primitive maenads had known?

One can only ask the question. No ancient author specifically attributes that particular kind of 'enthusiasm' to the Athenian audiences. But the Bacchic frenzy was notoriously infectious, and the music of the pipe was notoriously 'orgiastic'. The most likely time for audiences to feel it strongly would have been when one of the many tragedies and satyr plays on Dionysiac themes were being performed. Only one of these has survived, Euripides' *Bacchai*. Its potency for orgiastic excitement was vividly demonstrated at a production in New York in 1969 when actors, chorus and audience actively participated in an unrestrained orgy in the widest sense of that word, with much nudity and sexuality. Nothing so outrageous as that is attributable to the respectable citizens of ancient Athens during the tragic performances. But such excesses prove that the potentiality is, and was, there for the full force of the Dionysiac cult to break out, as it did later in Rome. And some of the Athenians would be aware of a close parallel between their situation in the theatre and a ceremony in an orgiastic cult similar to the cult of Dionysos. In the Corybantic rite of *thrónōsis* initiates were placed on a ceremonial throne and made to watch wild dancers whirling around them to the sound of a pipe until they, the initiates, were caught up in the *Schwärmerei* and, if need be, cured of their psychological troubles. Much has been made of this analogy by modern interpreters of the catharsis doctrine. But it is significant for the arousal of emotional excitement as well as for its assuagement.

Other features of the social background to the tragic performances must also have contributed to emotionalism. The fact that the Great Dionysia occurred only once a year ensured that anticipatory interest was stronger than it normally is now when theatres operate all the year round. (None of the greater tragedies, so far as is known, was performed at the other festivals of Dionysos.) The dramatists, actors, choruses, and choregists (the citizens who paid most of the expenses of the chorus), were familiar to the Athenians as fellow citizens and members of the several tribes and demes of the city. Consequently personal concern and tribal partisanship about the success of the teams competing for the prizes would be strong – of the same kind, if not of the same degree, as modern partisanship at a football match. The crowds, too, were of the size of our own attendances at sporting events. And the whole city was involved. Commerce was suspended. The law-courts and the Council-house were closed. Prisoners were released from jail to attend the ceremonies. Plato's estimate of more than 30,000 spectators in the Theatre of Dionysos (*Symposium* 175E) has been much doubted. But anyone who has been in an Athenian train or bus at rush hour will know how compressible Athenians can be, and the slopes of the Acropolis above the theatre are spacious. At any rate we must not think of the audience in terms of a few hundreds.

There was also the fact that the audiences were closely packed together. In our own theatres we are segregated and individualized in seats with dividing arms. If by accident we happen to touch a neighbouring stranger we apologize and hastily withdraw. Not so in ancient Athens. Most of the seats were narrow and had no arms, and the spectators were jam-packed, shoulder to shoulder and knee to knee. Standing

14

spectators would be closer still. If someone beside you sobbed or shuddered or trembled, you would feel it directly, and a wave of physical reaction could pass like an electric shock through all your neighbours. In this way the audience was a united group, a *thíasos*, not a collection of individuals. Mass emotionalism flourishes in compact crowds of that kind. An audience can become a mob, and emotion can become hysteria, as at Phrynichos' *Capture of Miletos*.

Since the tragic performances began early in the morning, the audiences were not composed of people fatigued from a day's work as so often in our theatres. As every lecturer knows, a morning class is generally much more alert and suggestible than classes in the afternoon or evening. As a result the Greek tragedians could expect a higher degree of attention, perception and participation, than a modern dramatist can.

The absence of any substantial barrier between the dancing-floor and the auditorium prevented that sense of separation – 'we' and 'they' – that prevails in a modern theatre of the conventional type, where the spectators are like hidden eaves-droppers observing the lives of others through the enormous keyhole of the proscenium arch. In Athens the actors and choruses could reach out and touch the front-row spectators, and in comedy they sometimes did. The shape of the Greek auditorium, going two-thirds of the way round the orchestra, strengthened the spatial continuity between cast and specta-tors. It is significant that recently built churches, as well as theatres, are often constructed in this shape, instead of in the rectangles of the basilican style, in order to bring congregations into closer involvement in the liturgy. For a similar reason the 'dim, religious light' of the Gothic style of church architecture is avoided. Congregations worship in full daylight like the Athenians on the southern slopes of the Acropolis. While darkness in church or theatre may promote awe and concen-tration, it encourages an individual response – individual piety, individual emotionalism. When you can see how your neigh-bours are responding, the emotionalism is shared and, in an emotional environment, increased.

Simplicity of scenery and stage properties would also help to concentrate the emotional effect of the drama itself. The elaborate and often changing scenery and lighting of modern theatres distract attention from the words and actions. They sometimes even win special rounds of applause, not for the dramatist or actors but for the stage manager and his team of artists, engineers, electricians and so many others. All that the Athenian spectator would see in the way of scenery was the scene-building painted to represent a palace, or temple, or cave, or something of the kind, and perhaps a separate representation of a tree on a rock or some object intended to symbolize the location rather than to create an illusion. (The nature of Sophocles' scenic innovations is unknown.) Unlike spectators in the architecturally enclosed theatres of the later period most of the audience would be able to see over the scene-building to the landscape of Attica – the slopes of Hymettos, the plain of Phaleron, and the Saronic Gulf beyond. This could be a distraction. But it was a familiar, extra-theatrical landscape. It did not call for attention like the contrived settings of our conventional theatres. The modern director may claim that his scenery and lighting can deepen the emotional impact of the drama. But the Greek dramatists, like Shakespeare, preferred to rely on the magic of the word to paint their scenery for them, as later chapters will illustrate.

The enormous size of the ancient Greek theatres might seem disadvantageous for *rapport* between performers and audiences. The spectators on the upper levels could be a hundred yards or more from the players, who would hardly seem bigger than puppets. Broad gestures would be visible, but facial expressions and subtle movements would be imperceptible. We who are used to large-scale figures and faces on cinema screens – with tears as large as footballs and frowns as big as pitchforks – might regard this as a sad loss of emotional expression. More will be said about this in a chapter on the visual aspects of tragedy, and especially about the use of masks. Here it needs only to be emphasized that, thanks to the superb acoustics of the Greek theatres and, one presumes, to the loud, clear voices of the players, the words and the music would reach even the more distant listeners, and it was the words and the music that supremely mattered for the emotional effects.

The Athenian audiences were not, like most of our theatre audiences, composed largely of intellectual and sophisticated citizens. All adult citizens – female perhaps as well as male, but the evidence is uncertain – were expected to attend – farmers, craftsmen, shopkeepers, manual labourers, in far greater numbers than the priests, poets, philosophers and sophists. These last might be chiefly interested in the intellectual aspects of the plays. But *hoi polloí* would be more inclined to emotionalism, like popular cinema audiences in our time. And the dramatists competing for the prize in democratic Athens would be well aware that a vote from a shoemaker was as good as a vote from a philosopher.

We are used to intervals between the acts in drama and sometimes in longer films. These interrupt the emotional tension and make a continuous crescendo towards a grand climax impossible. The Greek tragedies, so far as we know, were played without any break. When the poet-dramatist wished to relax the tension for a while he could do so by means of a quieter chorus. But there is a great difference between letting the audience go away to chatter in the foyer and, in contrast, soothing them by structurally relevant song, dance and music, in the auditorium. When in the later phases of classical drama the choruses became mere interludes it must have caused a decline in audience-control and in emotional suspense.

Concentration of feeling and attention were also helped by the convention that the scene of the tragic event was rarely changed and intervals of time within the plot were not emphasized. Even when, as in *Agamemnon* and *Eumenides*, extra-theatrical time must be assumed to elapse between successive scenes, psychologically the time-sequence is continuous. Similarly the occasional changes of scene, as in *Ajax* and *Eumenides*, resulted from exigencies of plot, not from a desire for variety. Most important of all, as in Aristotle so strongly asserted, was the unity of plot without diversions or sub-plots – a sustained continuum of beginning, middle and end. Such concentration could hardly be maintained in a modern play of over two hours' duration, much less during the full length of *Hamlet*, or *Faustus II*, or *Peer Gynt* or *Maria Stuart*. The length of the extant Greek tragedies ranges from 1,047 lines in *Eumenides* to 1,779 in *Oedipus at Colonos*. At the fairly fast rate of twenty lines a minute the longest would take no more than an hour and a half. Trilogies might have taken about four hours. But they had a separate climax in each play, even in the *Oresteia* where the theme is continuous.

Psychologists have suggested that complete attention cannot be sustained for more than about fifty minutes – university lecture time. If this is true the longer Greek tragedies would require a special effort from their audiences. But the Greek Dionysia came but once a year, like Christmas, and the accumulated emotional energy could have met the demand without strain.

Finally, what are the implications of the fact that most, if not all, of the audience knew about the tragic catastrophe beforehand? The amount of their knowledge has been disputed, since the two main sources of evidence seem to contradict each other. Aristotle in *Poetics* (145lb 25–6) asserts that 'the known things' in tragedy are 'known only to a few'. But Antiphanes, earlier in the fourth century than Aristotle, complained (fr. 191), as a writer of comedies, that the tragedians had an advantage because they used ready-made and familiar themes. Whatever we make of this contradiction – it presumably is a question of degree of knowledge, not of total familiarity or ignorance – one thing is hardly deniable: all but the most ignorant of the audience must have known from myths and epics what would be the outcome of plays on traditional subjects. The children of Thyestes must be partly eaten by their father. Agamemnon must be killed by his wife. Ajax must commit suicide. The Trojan women must be enslaved. Oedipus must discover his guilt. Details of time, place and method could vary. Occasionally a drastic alteration might be made in the tradition, as when Euripides adopted the notion that Helen never went to Troy. And some of the stories may have been unfamiliar or invented. But in such cases generally Euripides took care to tell the audience in his prologues or early dialogue what was going to happen. So it comes as no surprise when Heracles rescues Alcestis from Death. Apollo predicts it early in the play.

The contrast with modern drama of the more conventional kind is clear. In it suspense is modified to some extent by hope and uncertainty, while there was no hope and no uncertainty about the fate of the Greek tragic hero or heroine. Curiosity about the outcome of a plot is intellectually more stimulating than foreknowledge, but less emotive. Plays which encourage it approximate to the conditions of life with its uncertain future. The classical dramas conformed, instead, to the canons of art with its predestined end.

This element of suspense was a main factor in tragic emotionalism, and Aeschylus was a supreme master in it, as will be exemplified in a later chapter. Here perhaps an actual experience of the present writer may serve to emphasize the emotional effect of watching an unsuspecting victim advancing to certain death. In 1934 King Alexander of Yugoslavia was assassinated in Marseilles at the beginning of a state visit to France. His arrival and death were fully filmed by newsmen. When the newsreel came to Dublin everyone had already read accounts of the murder. So, with full foreknowledge of the imminent *páthos*, we watched the King's warship arriving at the port. We saw the King himself smiling and waving as he came down the gangway, while the crowds cheered and the bands played and the flags waved. He, like Agamemnon on his return, was totally unaware of his doom. Somewhere in the crowd the assassin knew that the attempt would soon be made. Only we of the audience were certain that it would succeed – but how and when?

More slowly than seemed natural, the King received the welcomes of the officials and entered an open car. By this time the suspense was agonizing. My hands were gripping the arms of the seat. I wished I could call out a warning. The car drove slowly on. The crowds cheered more wildly as the King responded happily to their Gallic enthusiasm. (Or so I remember it after many years: I have not been able to check these recollections with the film.) Suddenly the murderer rushed out of the crowd and shot the King dead. By then I was trembling with a mixture of pity and fear. But, since the film was a record of an actual event and not a work of high art, I felt no catharsis afterwards.

The analogies with a tragedy like *Agamemnon* are obviously close – a king arriving in an hour of triumph and festivity, the welcoming citizens, the music in the background, the stately advance towards death. (But in one way Agamemnon's fate was more pathetic. It came to him in his own home and from one who should have been nearest and dearest to him.) The fact that King Alexander's death occurred in such an aura of royal pomp and ceremony gave it – for me at least – greater emotional force than the death of President Kennedy in less ceremonious circumstances. In Dallas there was more cause for grief after the event. In Marseilles there was more scope for pity and fear before it.

When the unstructured suspense of a brief documentary film could have such a powerful effect – which I know was shared by others – how much stronger must have been the impact of a royal tragedy presented with supreme artistry of diction, gesture, rhythm, music and choreography, by a master dramatist in the precincts of a consecrated theatre!

CHAPTER THREE

The emotions of Greek tragedy

'By means of pity and fear effecting a catharsis of such emotions' – this desperately controversial statement by Aristotle in *Poetics* 1449b 27–8 (the given translation is only one of several possibilities) has tended to confine discussion of emotion in Greek tragedy to these two, with the occasional addition of anger, mentioned casually in *Poetics* 1456b 1. While it is true that they are dominant in Greek tragedy as we have it, they are certainly not the only emotions presented there, and they often gain in effectiveness by contrast with others. They may perhaps properly be described as 'the tragic emotions', but they are far from being the only emotions in tragedy.

Before considering the emotions presented in tragedy and felt by audiences it should be emphasized that apparently they were much more strongly visceral than is normal in more northern latitudes now. The tragedians describe the strongest of them, grief and fear, as being felt in the entrails, womb, liver, heart, midriff, lungs or head, like a stab, or a sting, or a bite, or a fire, or a chilling frost. They cause people to tear their flesh or hair (which stands on end in extreme emotion), to tremble and shudder, to fall prostrate, to become dumb or to utter inarticulate cries in a shrill voice – besides weeping, sobbing, groaning and wailing, sometimes for long periods. Perhaps the tragedians exaggerated this emotionalism for their own artistic purposes. But it is the normal climate of Greek tragedy.

Before considering the main definitions of the stronger passions in ancient Greece, one grave semantic difficulty must be recognized. As has been fully discussed elsewhere, the meaning of the word *psuchē* varies widely from the time of Homer onwards, ranging from a ghost, to a butterfly. The commonest translation in English, 'soul', with its spiritual and ethereal overtones, can be highly misleading in many tragic contexts, pre-Platonic as they are. Its salient meaning in tragedy is that faculty in human nature which feels and reacts to sensations and emotions. Heracles tells his father that he must force his *psuchē* to share his woes (*Heracles* 1366, cf. 626). The *psuchē* of the chorus in *Hippolytos* 173 passionately desires to learn what is the matter with their wan-faced Queen. In the same play (527), the chorus sings of how Eros brings a sweet delight to *psuchaí*. Here *psuchē* means 'the emotional self' as often elsewhere. In *Antigone* 176 it is clearly distinguished from thought and opinion. It can also, of course, mean the intellectual self, but more rarely in tragedy than lexicographers and editors suggest. It has in fact more in common with the modern psychologist's 'psyche' than with the 'soul' of the theologians and moralists. But in what follows here it will be italicized and given its accent to indicate its individuality of meaning in Greek. (Similarly the word *phrēn* and its plural *phrénes*, whose meaning varies from 'midriff' to 'mind', will not usually be translated.)

A corresponding uncertainty about another aspect of the emotions also arises here. How does one distinguish emotions from mental processes? Aristotle's criterion will be adopted in what follows in this chapter. In his treatise *On the Psuchē* (403a 4ff.) he observes that the emotions (*páthē*) all involve physical symptoms and that some observable bodily effect results from all of them. In his *Nicomachean Ethics* 1128b 10ff., for example, he discusses whether shame is an emotion and decides that it is because it is accompanied by a 'somatic' symptom, blushing, just as terror causes one to grow pale. This is clear enough, but obviously there are times when emotions merge into mental attitudes. In modern times we would hardly call 'boldness' (*thársos*) an emotion, as Aristotle does.

There are many other problems about the subtler aspects of ancient speculations on the nature of the emotions which are beyond the scope of the present study. Fortunately two recent studies have discussed them very fully from ethical and

psychological points of view. Attention here will be mainly
confined to literary questions and especially to the implications
of the advice that the ancient rhetoricians gave to practising
orators on how to work on the emotions of their audiences. As
already noticed, Greek oratory could be highly histrionic and
Greek drama strongly rhetorical at times, and, as a later chapter
will illustrate, both orators and dramatists constantly used the
same emotive figures of speech.

Aristotle's *Rhetoric* is our best helper in this. The first eleven
chapters of his second book are devoted to describing the chief
emotions that an orator can profitably evoke – anger, affection,
friendliness, enmity, hatred, fear, shame, pity, indignation and
others. (His discussions of these and other emotions in his two
Ethics are less pertinent to the present study.) In his *Rhetoric* he
gives pride of place and much of his attention to anger and its
associate emotions. But since pity and fear are the salient tragic
emotions in his *Poetics* we shall consider them first.

The supreme tragic emotion, to judge from the surviving
tragedies, is *éleos* or *oîktos*. Both words are generally translated
into English as 'pity', but the word is often inadequate to
express the visceral intensity of the Greek terms. *Éleos* may be
cognate with the ritual cry of grief and pain, *eleleû*, uttered by
Io in *Prometheus* 877 when agony seizes her. *Oîktos* is the
commoner word in tragedy. It may be derived from the regular
cry of woe, *oi*. It seems to be rather stronger in force than *éleos*.
If these etymologies are correct, both terms attest that the basic
expression of grief is oral, varying from totally inarticulate
sounds like sobs and groans to half-articulate exclamatory
cries, and finally to intelligible speech. As will be exemplified
in the next chapter, Greek had an extraordinarily wide range of
exclamatory semi-animalistic cries ('interjections') that are far
more visceral than our 'alas'. These cries and also the tragic
descriptions of *éleos* and *oîktos* imply agonies of feeling far
beyond the normal connotation of our word 'pity'. Our 'pity'
often implies a mental attitude rather than a visceral experience. The pitier tends to consider himself superior to the
pitied. As a result, it is generally considered rather wounding

to say 'I pity you', and many people in misfortune would prefer not to be pitied in that cerebral and detached way. 'Pity' can be used very casually too, as in Polonius's ' 'Tis true 'tis pity and pity 'tis 'tis true', where one would be ill-advised to translate 'pity' as *éleos* or *oîktos*.

'Compassionate grief' is perhaps the best rendering of these terms in many of their tragic contexts. There is no question here of the pitier being separate from another's agony. You respond to it in the depths of your being, as a harp-string responds by sympathetic resonance to a note from another source (as implied in the modern psychosomatic meaning of 'vibrations', 'vibes'). At climactic moments in tragedy this compassionate grief approaches that of the Mater Dolorosa as she laments over the dead body of her Son in traditional *Pietà* scenes. The same depth of physical feeling is expressed in the Greek versions of the Bible by a verb that indicates a sensation in one's entrails (*splanchnízō*), and in the phrase in I John 3, 17, translated in the Authorised Version as 'bowels of compassion'.

Aristotle uses the term *éleos*, not *oîktos*, in his *Rhetoric*. He defines *éleos* as a kind of pain (*lúpē*) felt at the sigh of a destructive or painful event happening to someone who does not deserve it – an evil and fearful event close at hand which one might expect to happen to oneself or to a relative or friend, *phílos*. The people likely to feel it most strongly are those who themselves have suffered and survived bad fortune – especially the aged, weak, timid, and those with parents, wives and children of their own – and also well-educated, intelligent people, as Orestes says in Euripides' *Electra* 294–5. On the other hand, *éleos* is less likely to affect people who are themselves in a desperate state or in a mood of arrogant self-confidence, or who are angry, rash, afraid or shocked. There is evidence that the ancient Athenians were strongly susceptible to appeals for compassion as well as being prone to fits of anger (Plutarch, *Moralia* 790C, Demosthenes 24,171). Cleon, according to Thucydides (3, 39, 2), found it necessary to warn them against the dangers of compassion towards enemies. The fifth-century painter Parrhasios placed Pity and Anger among the salient Athenian emotions in an allegorical painting (Pliny, *Natural History* 6, 35, 69). Callimachos (fr. 51, Pfeiffer) asserted 'Athens alone knows how to feel pity.' According to Pausanias (1, 17, 1), there was an altar of Pity in Athens (but it may have been post-classical). Thrasymachos, the fifth-century rhetorician and the villain of Plato's *Republic*, excelled in appeals to pity and wrote a treatise on them. Two late writers, Athenaios (13, 659E) and Quintilian (6, 1, 7), state that a law was passed in Athens prohibiting the introduction of pitiful witnesses into the law courts, such as tearful women and wailing children and pathetic old men. This has been doubted, but it would not have been out of character for the temperamental Athenians to pass such a law and then to revoke it. In extant tragedies Athenian compassion is best embodied in the person of Theseus, as he appears in *Oedipus at Colonos* and in Euripides' *Suppliant Women*, *Heracles* and *Children of Heracles*.

Aristotle and later rhetoricians (especially Apsines 12, 392, 20) give lists of conditions that should arouse *éleos* in an audience, either when visually displayed in the persons of witnesses introduced for that purpose, or else when described by the orator (using the emotive devices that will be examined in chapter 7). These 'tear-jerkers' include poverty (especially after previous prosperity), sickness, old age, wounds, physical disabilities and deformities, mutilations, ugliness, hunger, exile, dishonour, loneliness, loss of *phíloi*, captivity, abduction, childlessness, orphanhood, outrage and death – all of which except hunger are fully exploited by the tragedians. Circumstances could intensify the emotional effect, when, for example, death comes to young, unmarried women (like Antigone, Iphigeneia and Macaria) or to people in the prime of life (like the Greek warriors so pathetically praised and mourned in *Agamemnon*), or to helpless infants (as in *Medea* and *Heracles*), or when people past child-bearing are deprived of children or grandchildren (like Cadmos and Peleus), or when noble figures are painfully deformed (like Oedipus and Philoctetes). Tragedy thrives on situations of that kind.

Euripides is specially adept in presenting pitiful scenes between parents and children, husbands and wives, and brothers and sisters, old and young, with tender, protracted embraces and copious tears. Aeschylus has no young children on-scene in his extant plays (though the Nurse in *Libation-bearers* gives a poignant description of Orestes as an infant) and he only exploits the pathos of old age briefly in *Agamemnon* 72–82. Sophocles lies between the two in this respect. In one play in which he uses a child as a major adjunct to a pitiful scene – Eurysakes in *Ajax* – he does so very effectively, but the focus is on Ajax not on the boy. Sophocles' most pitiful figure in many respects is his Electra, as the scholia on 190, 260, 516 and 827 imply. He exhibits the sorrows of old age most movingly in *Oedipus at Colonos*, and those of virginal death in *Antigone*.

Aristotle implies that there is often an element of self-pity in 'pity'. (The normal English term will be used here with the previous qualifications in mind.) The classic example of this is in *Iliad* 19, 302, where the captive women in Achilles' tent join in the lamentations over the corpse of Patroclos, but, Homer adds, 'It was a pretext, for each was bewailing her own personal sorrows.' This is also true of many expressions of compassionate grief by choruses in tragedy, especially when the singers are captive women or servants. Male choruses, as in *Agamemnon*, are less inclined to voice self-pity in their grief. But often one cannot clearly separate pity, self-pity and grief, among tragic characters. The pity of audiences can be complicated in the same way, as in the Athenians' reaction to Phrynichos' *Capture of Miletos* (and cf. on *Agamemnon* 452 ff.)

The tragedians also exploited an emotion that was akin to pity but milder, more abstract and more cerebral – *philanthrōpía*, 'love of humanity'. In contrast with pity which is chiefly directed towards individuals this emotion, or sentiment, was concerned with humanity in general, but more warmly, it seems, than our 'philanthropy' and almost approaching the Christian concept, 'charity'. The noun does not appear in Greek tragedy, but the adjective is applied to Prometheus by Kratos ('Force') in *Prometheus* – unfavourably since Kratos being an accomplice of tyrannous Zeus does not approve of his 'mankind-loving disposition'. Prometheus is the great exemplar of *philanthrōpía* in extant tragedy, though in *Prometheus* itself the dominant passions are anger against Zeus and self-pity. Odysseus also provides a noble example of this philanthropic pity in *Ajax* 121–6 when Ajax has just been exhibited in his madness by the vindictive Athene. Refusing to gloat over his defeated enemy he exclaims:

> . . . I pity him
> In his utter distress, though he's an enemy,
> Yoked as he is to catastrophic fate.
> And here I see myself as much as him.
> I know that we are nothing more in all our life
> Than feeble images or fragile shades.

Later Odysseus briefly repeats this sentiment of common humanity with his enemy when he is trying to persuade Agamemnon to allow the burial of Ajax (1338). It resembles the feeling expressed by John Bradford when he saw a criminal being led to execution, 'But for the grace of God there goes John Bradford.' Theseus shows the same attitude in a more general way in *Oedipus at Colonos* and in Euripides' *Suppliant Women* (549–63), and it sometimes underlies reflections on human life elsewhere. Perhaps its most moving appearance in tragedy is when Cassandra in her last words transcends her feelings of self-pity and hate with a pitiful and pitying description of the fragility of human fortunes, as will be noticed again in chapter 9.

While pity is mostly altruistic, fear is generally self-centred. Fear is the stronger emotion in the sense that it can drive out pity, as Aristotle observes. Fear is generally concerned with the future, pity with the past or present. Aristotle defines it as a painful feeling (*lúpē*) or disturbance (*tarachē*) caused by the visualization (*phantasía*) of a destructive event in the near future. The commonest word for it, *phóbos* (which Aristotle

27

uses) implies an instinct to run away. Two other terms, *déos* and *deîma* seem to have been less strongly emotional. *Phóbos* is personified in the *Iliad* and *Theogony* and twice by Aeschylus (in *Seven against Thebes* 45 and 500, *v.l*). Our word 'fear' is a less inadequate translation for *phóbos* than 'pity' for *éleos*, but 'terror' is often more apt for it in tragedy. Milder and more cerebral forms are apprehension and anxiety (*mérimna, tárbos*, and *phrontís*).

The symptoms of fear as described by rhetoricians and dramatists are – in ascending order of intensity – paleness, chilliness, a fast pulse, shivering, shuddering, shrieking, hair standing on end, prostration. It is felt in the same organs as compassionate grief, but it affects them more violently at times, as when Io's heart 'kicks' against her midriff in sudden fear in *Prometheus* 881. There is no reference to its being felt in the head (unlike grief in *Medea* 144 and *Hippolytos* 1351). Like anger and *érōs* it approaches madness at times. Aristotle emphasizes that people do not fear remote and general things but things close at hand and threatening great pain or harm. Even the signs of such things are fearful (one thinks of the noise of the attackers in *Seven against Thebes* or the blood-red fabrics in *Agamemnon*). Fear, if it is not overwhelming, makes people take counsel, but only when some hope of escape remains. When an orator wants to make his audience feel fear he should make them think that they themselves are likely to suffer, by showing that more powerful people have suffered and that people like themselves have suffered unexpectedly. These are Aristotle's views.

Sudden fright, however, could cause a state of shock and stupefaction called *ékplēxis*, literally a 'knocking out'. In it the impact of a pitiable or fearful sight is so strong as to have a paralysing effect: one is 'frozen stiff'. Aristotle tells how King Amasis of Egypt wept when he saw a friend begging in the streets but did not weep when he saw his son being led to execution: the first sight was pitiable, the second terrible (*deinón*). Tennyson portrays the same reaction in a song in his 'Princess':

Home they brought her warrior dead:
She nor swoon'd, nor utter'd cry:
All her maidens, watching, said,
'She must weep or she will die'.

Aristotle mentions dramatic *ékplēxis* three times in *Poetics* (1454a 4, 1455a 17, and 1460b 25). In the first passage, discussing recognitions, he says that to do the deed in ignorance and then to recognize the victim as a *phílos* causes *ékplēxis*. In the second he claims that the best recognition is one that emerges logically from the action, as in *King Oedipus* and *Iphigeneia among the Taurians*. In the third he argues that physical improbabilities in an episode such as the pursuit of Hector in *Iliad* 22 are tolerable when it has *ékplēxis*. In the first two examples the term means little more than surprise, but in the third it implies an overwhelming emotional effect. It is used in its strongest force in the *Life of Aeschylus* where it is stated that Aeschylus used his visual effects to create spectacular *ékplēxis*, and the same word is used in connection with the panic at the appearance of the Erinyes in *Eumenides*. In tragedy *ékplēxis* generally refers to the paralysing effect of intense fear. But it can also be the result of passionate *érōs* as with Phaidra in *Hippolytos* 38 and Medea in her first encounter with Jason (as described in *Medea* 8) when her spirit was 'shattered with love', or with Electra in *Libation-bearers* 233 when her heart is 'overwhelmed with pleasure' at Orestes' return.

A less overwhelming result of emotional stress is *taraché* (also *táragma* and *taragmós*), 'confusion'. Plato in *Laws* 632a says that it comes to the *psuché* from fear or anger. It is fear that makes Oedipus exclaim 'What a wandering of my *psuché* and upheaval of my *phrénes* possesses me' after he had heard that Laios was killed at a junction of three roads (*King Oedipus* 727). It can also be caused by remorse and a sense of guilt – or at least the chorus think so – when Orestes becomes violently agitated after killing his mother (*Libation-bearers* 1056), and by *érōs* (*Hippolytos* 181–85) or pity (*Hecuba* 850–7). *Taraché*

29

varies in tragedy from mental confusion involving perplexity, indecision and hesitation, to a deeply felt visceral feeling as described by the chorus in *Agamemnon* 1025–34.

Euripides shows special skill in presenting *taraché* as a prelude to, or an aftermath of, madness. In *Heracles* 929–30 the hero falls silent and stops his action, as signs of his confusion, before he goes berserk (cf. 836 and 533). Later (1091–3) he exclaims 'I have fallen into a surge and confusion (*tarágmati*) of my *phrénes*: I breathe out hot breaths slowly, not silently, from my lungs.' In the brilliant scene towards the end of *Bacchai* (1264 ff.) when Cadmos helps Agave to recover from her Dionysiac frenzy he asks her 'Is the fluttering feeling still in your *psuché*?' At first Agave fails to understand him, but she feels a change in her *phrénes*. Just before the final revelation that it was she herself who killed her son, her *taraché* turns to fearful apprehension – 'My heart leaps with regard to what is coming.' The 'fluttering' of *taraché* has now been focused on a specific fear. Then the appalling revelation comes to her with shattering force.

Aristotle gives pride of place and by far the most space in his *Rhetoric* to anger and its cause, which, according to Plutarch (*Moralia* 790C), was a proclivity (besides pity) of the Athenians. Presumably this means that he believed it to be the most effective weapon in the orators' emotional armoury. Its pedigree in literature goes back to the first word in the *Iliad*, *mênis*, the most heavily charged term for anger in Greek, implying a long-lasting rancorous passion (cf. Zeno in Diogenes Laertius, *Lives of Philosophers*, 7, 114). That whole poem is a study in the calamitous results of divine and human wrath. Achilles, the supremely wrathful hero, describes the paradoxical pleasure brought by *chólos* (a more visceral term for anger, cf. *cholé*, 'gall'): 'It is much sweeter than honey, and it swells in the bosom of men like smoke' (*Iliad* 18, 109–10), a passage quoted by Plato in a discussion of the mixture of pleasure and pain that one feels in some emotions (*Philebos* 47E). The comparison to smoke swelling up from a fire is specially apt for the commonest term for anger, *orgé*, since it is cognate with a verb meaning to swell and probably also with the Greek word for 'orgy' (in which one swells with passion and excitement). Another word, *kótos*, implies smouldering rancour or resentment rather than blazing rage. (*Thumós* will be noticed later.)

Aristotle describes *orgḗ* in his *Rhetoric* as a desire, accompanied by *lúpē*, for revenge as a result of a slight or injury to oneself or to a *phílos*, when the slight or injury is undeserved – a rather narrow definition but characteristic of the love of personal honour (*tò philótimon*) among the ancient and modern Greeks (cf. *Iphigeneia at Aulis* 22 and Euripides' *Suppliant Women* 907). In *De Anima* 403b 1 he says that physicians attribute it to a boiling (*zésis*) of the blood (as in our phrase 'It makes my blood boil') or heat round the heart. Seneca in his long and eloquent essay on anger quotes Aristotle (from an unknown source: see Rose fr. 80) as asserting that anger was a necessary and serviceable emotion: without it one cannot win contests and conflicts: it fills the mind and fires the spirit: but it must serve as a subordinate soldier not as a commander (*De Ira* 1, 9, 2, cf. 3, 3, 1). This is the *thumós* of Homer's heroes.

Such was the orthodox Peripatetic view of the passions – good servants but bad masters. A severer view was taken by the Platonists with their intellectualism, by the Stoics with their freedom from passion (*apátheia*), and by the Epicureans with their freedom from disturbance (*ataraxía*). Seneca as a good Stoic – and perhaps because Roman anger was more terrible than Greek – condemned uncontrolled anger as 'a brief madness' (*brevis insania*), and the most disgusting and most frenzied (*maxime . . . taetrum ac rabidum*) of all the emotions (*De Ira* 1, 1–2). He, in contrast with Aristotle in *Rhetoric*, is concerned as a moral philosopher with preventing anger entirely, not with suggesting ways of stimulating it among audiences. He finds it easy to cite examples of its disastrous consequences (and those of our time who have witnessed what anger and hate can do in national politics could easily surpass them).

Just how violent angry rage could be in antiquity can be seen in Seneca's descriptions of a furiously angry man (*De Ira* 1, 1, 4, and 3, 4, 1).

> His eyes blaze and flash, his whole face is reddened with the blood that surges up from the depths of his heart, his lips quiver, his hair bristles and stands on end, his teeth are clenched, his breathing is forced and harsh, a sound comes from his writhing limbs, there are groanings and bellowings and his speech is abrupt and scarcely intelligible, he frequently strikes his hands together and stamps the ground with his feet, his whole body is excited. . . .
>
> His face is now sharp and fierce and pale from the withdrawal and dispersal of blood, now suffused with red as if steeped in gore when all the heat and force has turned back into it. His veins swell. His eyes are sometimes restless and darting, now fixed in a single stare and unmoving. And add the sound of clashing teeth, . . . the creaking of joints when his hands crush each other, the pulsation of his breast, his rapid breathing and deep-drawn groans, his unsteady body, his faltering speech and sudden outcries, with lips now trembling and now tight and hissing out some terrible phrase.

Aristotle offers nothing as sensational as this in his discussion of *orgē*. *Orgē*, he says, is always directed towards individuals, not towards people in general. Though a *lúpē*, it contains a certain pleasure resulting from the hope of revenge. It is caused by experiencing contempt, spite, hindrance or insult (in the form of injury, annoyance or dishonour), and by damage to one's self-esteem rather than physical pain. People become specially angry at being ill-treated by their friends or beneficiaries (ingratitude and disloyalty). Those who desire something and cannot obtain it are 'prone to anger and easily excited', including the victims of *érōs*. So, too, the disappointed, the ridiculed, the deprived, the victims of irony or of indifference. 'It is clear, then', Aristotle concludes, 'that it

will be necessary for the speaker by his speech to put his
hearers into the psychological condition of those who are
inclined to anger, and to show that his opponents are responsible for things that deserve anger and are the kind of people
with whom men are angry.'

Much of this is applicable to what the tragedians made of
angry characters in their plays, like Oedipus, Creon, Medea,
Eteocles, Pentheus, Artemis, Aphrodite, Athene (in *Ajax*),
and Dionysos. If one seeks an Aristotelian *hamartía* (as in
Poetics 1453a 9ff.) to explain the calamities of 'decent' tragic
heroes and heroines, one finds anger the most probable in
many cases. It brings disaster to Creon, Ajax, Theseus (in
Hippolytos) and Pentheus. It has the advantage over other
faults of being characteristically heroic, arising from the
thumós (sometimes used as a synonym for *orgé*) which was the
steam, so to speak, in the engine of the heroic temperament.
Zeno, as quoted above, called it 'anger at its outset'.

Anger often merges into hate. Aristotle distinguishes the
two in several ways. Hate can be focused on classes as well as
individuals – 'Everyone hates a thief or an informer.' Time
cures anger but not hatred. Anger aims at causing pain, hate at
causing harm in general. An angry man can feel compassion,
but one who hates cannot. There is some feeling of pain in
being angry, but not in hating. Among the outstanding haters
in tragedy are Clytemnestra and Cassandra (in *Agamemnon*),
Electra, Ajax, Oedipus (at Colonos), and Hermione. The
dialogue at the end of *Medea* (1323–9), when Medea has done
her worst, illustrates how virulent a mixture of anger and hate
can be. Jason denounces her:

> O thing of hate (*mîsos*), O woman most greatly most-
> odious [*echthístē*: this kind of hyperbole in passionate
> speech will be considered in chapter 7] to the gods and me,
> you who dared to thrust a sword against your children,
> you who destroyed me by depriving me of my children –
> after such impious deeds do you still look upon the sun
> and earth? May you perish. . . .

Sometimes an element of loathing and revulsion (*stúgos*) is involved in hatred, as in Cassandra's attitude to Clytemnestra in *Agamemnon*. Its most forceful non-verbal expression is spitting, as in *Antigone* 1232, *Hippolytos* 614, *Helen* 664, *Heracles* 560, and *Hecuba* 1276. (This can also be an apotropaic gesture.) An aesthetic element is involved here, the object of disgust being regarded as obscene, or abominable, or monstrous, as when Artemis is said to loathe the feasting of the eagles on the pregnant hare and its brood (*Agamemnon* 137) and when the Erinyes are described as 'spitting away' the adultery of Thyestes with his brother's wife (*Agamemnon* 1192). The chorus of Erinyes in *Eumenides* provide the paramount example of a mixture of the loathsome, the abominable, the horrible and the terrifying. (Horror is perhaps to be distinguished from terror by an aesthetic quality, and it also tends to paralyse and transfix, while terror, as *phóbos* implies, incites panic flight. As will be noticed again later, the Gorgon was the chief emblem of paralysing horror in ancient Greece.)

Two other emotions akin to anger, one virtuous, the other vicious, are described in full in *Rhetoric* – justified indignation (*némesis*) and envious spite (*phthónos*). *Némesis*, connected with a verb meaning 'to apportion' was embodied at the highest religious level in the dread goddess of the temple at Rhamnous in Attica who struck down those who exceeded the limits of appropriate behaviour, as in *Philoctetes* 518. On the human level *némesis* meant being pained at another's undeserved good fortune, or sometimes at someone's bad conduct (as in *Oedipus at Colonos* 1753). Like pity, it is a virtuous quality. 'No good man', Aristotle affirms, 'would be pained when parricides and foul murderers are punished: on the contrary such just actions cause a reasonable man to be glad.' (There were no John Bradfords in his time, it seems.) So, Aristotle concludes, if an orator wants to prevent his audience from feeling pity he should make them feel *némesis* – as the tragedians did in portraying Clytemnestra, Aigisthos and Lycos.

The other chief enemy of pity, as Aristotle observes, is spiteful envy (*phthónos*) which is the kind of *lúpē* felt by a malicious person (or god) at the prosperity of others who deserve it. In tragedy it is mainly confined to the gods. Since to possess *phthónos* in a high degree would make a person villainous, tragic figures do not show it strongly. But it is involved in the sexual jealousy of Clytemnestra, Deianeira, Hermione and Medea. The corresponding feeling, *epichairekakía, Schadenfreude*, pleasure at another's grief and pain (cf. *Rhetoric* 1379b 17 and *Nicomachean Ethics* 1107a 10 ff.) is also exemplified occasionally. In *Heracles* 731–3 Amphitryon announces that he will go and look at the corpse of Lycos because there is pleasure in the death of an enemy, and Electra, Medea, Hecuba and Alcmene exult in the deaths of their enemies, even though Odysseus had asserted so emphatically in *Odyssey* 22, 412, that it was impious to do so. Fear of giving a similar pleasure to enemies motivates Cassandra in *Agamemnon* 1271–2, Megara and Heracles in *Heracles* 285 and 1287–90, Ajax in *Ajax* 392, and others. Aristotle implies that Greek audiences were prone both to *phthónos* and *epichairekakía*. It has been suggested that in the lost second book of his *Poetics* the comic catharsis was of these two emotions.

Aristotle devotes over what amounts to five octavo pages of print to shame (*aischúnē*). He defines it as a kind of *lúpē* or *tarachḗ* with regard to misdeeds bringing dishonour which are perpetrated by oneself or by people one cares for, such as throwing away one's shield in battle, withholding a deposit, illicit sexual intercourse, exploiting the weak or poor, cadging money from people poorer than oneself, and much else. Phaidra is tragedy's saddest victim of shame. The bitter shame of great heroes like Ajax and Heracles results from their great *philótimon*. Clytemnestra in *Agamemnon* is the paragon of shamelessness.

Aischúnē can mean shame before or after a dishonourable deed. Its companion *aidṓs* is the sense of reverence for accepted good principles of conduct that prevents people from doing shameful actions (though occasionally it comes after the deed). *Aidṓs* (not specifically discussed in *Rhetoric* but see *Nicomachean Ethics* 1108a 32) is personified with Nemesis in

Hesiod's *Works and Days* 200, that pessimistic passage describing their departure from earth in the Age of Iron, and she had an altar in Athens according to Hesychios.

The subtlest and most varied presentation of *aidós* is in *Hippolytos* where all three leading characters are affected by it, Hippolytos in 78, Phaidra in 244 and 335, and Theseus in 1258. First we meet Aidos personified by Hippolytos as the gardener of a pure springtime grove where only those who are naturally temperate and chaste can gather flowers – an ominous prelude to the revelation of the Queen's guilty passion. Phaidra in turn is tortured by a conflict between *érōs* and *aidós* (cf. the scholium on 386). Then, when her passion is revealed to her stepson, the shame of it leads her to suicide, like Jocasta in *King Oedipus*. Consequently, Hippolytos dies as the result of the anger of Theseus, because *aidós* has prevented him from breaking his oath. Elsewhere in tragedy *aidós* means respect for venerable figures or compassionate regard for people in trouble (cf. *Persians* 699, *Oedipus at Colonos* 247, *Suppliant Women* 911).

In Phaidra we see *aidós* in conflict with one of the most destructive of human passions, *érōs*, a term which covers all intense and passionate desire but is mainly confined to sexual objects. Eros appears as one of the primordial beings in the cosmos, 'fairest among the immortal gods and men, loosener of limbs, who tames their minds and the wise counsel in their breasts' in Hesiod's *Theogony* 120–2. The other divine patron of sexual passion, Aphrodite, rose from the foam later (191–3). Her companions in Hesiod are Eros and 'beautiful Desire' (Hímeros). In the classical period Aphrodite, who had several cults in Athens, became the supreme symbol of *érōs*. Later the great cosmic Eros became trivialized as a cupid. But in tragedy he retains much of his cosmic power.

While sexuality was generally accepted as a natural and enjoyable thing in classical antiquity, strong erotic passion was regarded as a sickness of mind and body, as both characters and choruses attest in tragedy. Irresistible sexual desire is the subject of several magnificent choruses (e.g. *Libation-bearers*

585ff., *Antigone* 781 ff., *Medea* 627ff., *Hippolytos* 525ff.). But it is generally regarded as something to be avoided not encouraged.

In tragedy *érōs* affects women most strongly (though *thelukratés* in *Libation-bearers* 600 must, I think, mean 'holding sway through women' as well as 'holding sway over women'). Though men feel *érōs* (e.g. Menelaos and Paris), in the sense of wishing to possess another, they are not portrayed as its tragic victims, but some of the gods are notorious addicts. The most vivid description of a woman's passionate *érōs* is in Sappho's *Ode to Anactoria*. As she gazes on her beloved, her voice fails her, her tongue grows rigid, a fiery sensation runs under her flesh, her eyes grow blind, her ears hum, sweat flows freely over her, her whole body trembles, she is paler than withered grass (or greener than fresh grass), and she seems almost to be dead. Perhaps this description is exaggerated for poetic effect, though Sappho is usually very sincere. But in any case, unless it were to some extent based on what people knew about erotic symptoms it would have been ridiculed rather than praised. The same principle holds for the fictitious Simaitha in Theocritos' second *Idyll* (88–90) when she confesses that her skin turned bright yellow, all her hair fell out, and she shrank to skin and bone, for love of a glamorous athlete. Plato does not hesitate to describe the shuddering, sweating and glowing of an initiate when he beholds absolute beauty (*Phaidros* 251 A–B).

In contrast with the explicit erotic scenes depicted on Greek vases, the references to sexual activities by pre-classical and classical poets (apart from satirists and comedians) are generally delicate. They normally are expressed only by terms meaning 'bed-chamber', 'bed' or 'couch' or 'the gifts of golden Aphrodite', or by symbolic imagery. (A few possible exceptions will be noticed in chapter 9.) Homer had set a high standard of restraint and delicacy in descriptions of sexual affairs. He describes three erotic scenes (*Iliad* 3, 441ff., 14, 292ff., and *Odyssey* 8, 267ff.), but without any anatomical details. He, like the tragedians, preferred to express the effects of amorous passion rather than its mechanisms, though perhaps lost poems about such victims of inhuman *érōs* as Pasiphaë and Leda may have been less reserved.

Aeschylus in *Frogs* 1043–55 accuses Euripides of introducing lovesick wives like Phaidra and Sthenoboia (in a lost play) as 'prostitutes'. (Perhaps Phaidra was less modest in the earlier version of *Hippolytos*.) It is true that there is nothing in the extant plays of Aeschylus and Sophocles to equal Euripides' characteristically full and subtle portrait of love-sick Phaidra, but *érōs* enters into the characterization of Clytemnestra, Cassandra, Helen, Menelaos and Antigone. Euripides, with his special interest in psychosomatic reactions, mentions many symptoms of Phaidra's condition (198–296): faintness, a sense of heaviness in her head, violent bodily movement, thirst, desire for rest, wild speech, desire to run free, a feeling of mental derangement, shame, tears, a sullen face and a refusal to reply to requests. All this turns to fierce anger when she learns how the Nurse has betrayed her (682ff.). And then she kills herself in shame and despair.

The Greeks had other words to describe less passionate kinds of 'love'. *Storgé* and its verb *stérgo* meant affection between close relatives – parents and children, brothers and sisters, husbands and wives. *Storgé* is normal for all such characters in tragedy. Alcestis, Tecmessa, and Deianeira, are outstanding in their affection for their husbands, Electra and Antigone for their fathers and brothers, Oedipus and Hecuba for their children. Notable exceptions who show hate rather than affection towards their *phíloi* are Clytemnestra, Medea and Oedipus (towards his sons at Colonos). Often a large measure of self-interest is involved, as Euripides plainly exhibits in his characterization of Admetos in *Alcestis*. Though he loves his wife dearly, he has no qualms in allowing her to die in his place. He bewails his misfortune in having to live without her and denounces his aged parents for not being willing to die instead. In the beautifully contrived final scene Admetos is made to speak of his *érōs* for his wife and to say that life offers him no pleasure without her, while she, veiled and unrecognized, listens (1080–4). After he has recognized her, his joy is so great that Heracles has to warn him against incurring the *phthónos* of the gods. His subsequent thanks to Heracles for delivering her from death well illustrate a minor emotion of tragedy, gratitude, *cháris* (discussed by Aristotle in *Rhetoric* 2, 7).

The signs of *storgē* in tragedy are: kissing on the head, eyes or lips, touching, caressing, embracing, tears or smiles. Euripides is ridiculed in *Frogs* 1322 for his fondness for depicting tender embraces between affectionate relatives. But some of his scenes of this kind are uniquely poignant, for example Andromache's farewell to her son in *Trojan Women* 740–9 and Medea's to her children in *Medea* 1071–80. One detail mentioned in both scenes is not found elsewhere, the sweet aroma of the children's soft flesh. Tragic feeling is increased in *Heracles* as well as in *Medea* by the fact that the beloved children will soon be killed by their parents.

Storgē was regarded as a duty as well as a virtue. The Greeks recognized this by using the verb *stérgo* in the sense 'put up with', as when Lichas in *Women of Trachis* 486 advises Deianeira to put up with her rival Iole, when Clytemnestra says she wishes 'to put up with these things, even though they are hard to bear' (*Agamemnon* 1570), and when Force tells Prometheus that he must learn how to put up with the tyranny of Zeus (*Prometheus* 10–11). The term *anankaîoi*, literally 'compulsory people', as applied to close relatives (e.g. in *Alcestis* 533 and *Andromache* 671) implies a similar sense of duty rather than of affection, and so, too, the term *kêdos* meaning 'kin' and 'care'. There is the same implication in the verb used twice in tragedy (see Euripides, *Suppliant Women* 764, and *Helen* 937), *agapô*, which also can mean 'I put up with'.

A more general term embracing all degrees of 'love' from passion to friendship was *philía*, a virtue and condition prized very highly by the ancient Greeks and Romans. Aristotle devotes two books to it in his *Nicomachean Ethics* and one in his *Eudemian Ethics*, and Plato's *Lysis* and Cicero's *De*

Amicitia discuss the same theme. Aristotle defines it in *Rhetoric* 2, 4, as wishing someone to have the things which we believe to be good and doing our best to get them for him. *Philía* must be mutual: *phíloi* should have the same notions of good and bad, and should love and hate the same persons.

Philía in the sense of friendship was traditionally exemplified in the person of Pylades who accompanies Orestes in *Libation-bearers* and in Euripides' *Electra*. But he speaks only three lines in the first and is a silent figure in the second. The other proverbial friend of a hero in antiquity, Peirithoos, does not appear with Theseus. But references to *philía* and *phíloi* in the widest sense are numerous in all three tragedians.

A milder form of *érōs* is *póthos*, that is, yearning for someone or something unobtainable or far away – the 'much-grieving *póthos*' that Gorgias in *Helen* ranked with pity and fear as a salient emotional effect of the spoken word. It is personified by Aeschylus as a child of Aphrodite in *Suppliant Women* 1039–40 and by Euripides as a companion of the Graces in *Bacchai* 413–14. Its objects range from food (*Orestes* 189) to children (*Helen* 1306, *Suppliant Women* 1088, and cf. Sophocles, *Electra* 544–5), and even death (*Andromache* 824). But it is commonest with an erotic or conjugal reference. The Persian wives yearn for their husbands in *Persians* 133. Menelaos yearns for Helen, now 'over the ocean', in *Agamemnon* 414. Both Deianeira and Heracles are its victims in the triangular conflicts of *Women of Trachis* (103ff., 368, 431, 632).

Euripides presents two varieties of *póthos* in *Hippolytos*. He introduces the theme with a vague, mystical passage spoken by the Nurse after the chorus have asked her about their lovelorn mistress (191–7):

> whatever else there is that is dearer than life, darkness
> hides it in clouds. We appear as unsatisfied lovers
> (*dusérōtes*) of this thing that gleams over the earth,
> through inexperience of another way of life and through
> concealment of the things below the earth. We are vainly
> borne on by stories.

This sounds almost nonsensical, and editors have suspected that it is an interpolation. But as an introduction to the *póthos* of Phaidra for escape to the wild regions of the countryside it offers a kind of sublimation of that kind of yearning, suggesting that behind it lies a mystical desire for 'the light that never was on sea or land', an almost neo-platonic concept. Elsewhere in Greek literature and history *póthos* sometimes has this mystical aura.

The more ordinary kind of *póthos*, the desire to be somewhere else or with someone else, dominates the early part of *Hippolytos*. When Phaidra first appears she expresses (209ff.) a wish to escape from her home to the countryside where streams of pure water flow and poplar trees cast a restful shade over the long grasses of the fields, or else – and here her deepest *póthos* begins to reveal itself – to the wooded mountainside where hunting hounds pursue the dappled deer. Her yearnings focus more closely – but unconsciously perhaps – on their ultimate goal when she prays to Artemis (the patron goddess of Hippolytos) to let her join the drivers of chariots on the beach – a place that Hippolytos frequents after his hunting (cf. 110–12). But her *póthos* ends, and *érōs* takes its place when she confronts Hippolytos himself.

Sometimes *póthos* in tragedy is less specific in its object, approximating more to the concept of escapism, the Psalmist's mood when he exclaimed 'Oh for the wings of a dove that I might fly away and be at rest.' The chorus in *Oedipus at Colonos* 1081–4 use the same image when they sing, 'Would I were a swift-bodied dove borne on the strong breeze to release my eye from the sky-high cloud of my struggles.' The Danaids in *Suppliant Women* 792–8 pray to escape to some place in the sky among the snowy clouds or else to a 'sheer, goat-deserted, unidentified, lonely-hearted, hanging, vulture-haunted rock' where their lustful pursuers could not reach them. The chorus in *Bacchai* 402ff. are geographically more precise. They yearn to leave the hostility of Pentheus in Thebes and to go to Cyprus or Macedonia.

An alternative way of escaping trouble is to try to send it

away (*apopompḗ*), as exemplified in Clytemnestra's wish in *Agamemnon* 1568ff. that the Daimon of the accursed house of Atreus could depart, and the desire of the chorus in *Heracles* 649–54 that hateful old age would be sunk under the waves of the sea or else be carried on wings to the upper air. Such expressions are more in the nature of a prayer than of an emotion, but they generally contain an element of negative *póthos*.

The reverse of wishing to escape is the commonly expressed *póthos* for one's native land. Homer set a pattern for exilic feeling of that kind when he portrayed Odysseus on the island of Calypso yearning with groans and tears to return home to Ithaca (*Odyssey* 5, 151–58: *nóstos* there is the origin of 'nostalgia'). Many of the characters and choruses in Greek tragedy (for example the Herald and Cassandra in *Agamemnon* 539–40 and 1157–9) express this nostalgia. As a general theme it runs through all Greek and Latin classical literature from Homer to Ovid and beyond. For more recent times one thinks of Joachim du Bellay's *Les Regrets* and Browning's *Home-thoughts from Abroad*. In Greek yearnings of this kind a recurrent formula is *eíthe genoímēn*, as recalled in Rupert Brooke's exilic poem about his home:

> *Eithe genoimen* . . . would I were
> In Grantchester, in Grantchester!

A feeling of love and admiration for one's native land (*philopatría*) was sometimes the source of this yearning. This patriotism also motivated such praise of Athens as one finds in *Oedipus at Colonos* (688–769 where Sophocles' own deme is praised) and in Euripides' *Children of Heracles*, *Suppliant Women*, and *Medea*. But except among exiles it is more a sentiment than a visceral emotion.

In direct contrast to the painful emotions described in the previous pages joy is an unmixed pleasure. It plays a major part in tragedy in two ways. It may be transient and, like a tragic victim, doomed to destruction, or it may be terminal in 'the happy ending'. Prodicos, the sophist, discoursed on it in the fifth century at Athens (Aristotle *Topics* 112b 22), but no extensive discussion has survived from antiquity. The Greeks had a strong capacity for joy (*chará*), delight (*térpsis*) and gladness (*euphrosúne*). Their liveliest expression was in the dance, as the name of the Muse Terpsichore implies. The chief symbols of joy in Greek poetry were light, the eye, and soaring aloft. Moments of joy are used in tragedy to provide *chiaroscuro* with prevailing grief. All three tragedians exemplify this technique, Aeschylus in *Agamemnon* (see chapter 9) and in *Libation-bearers* 235ff., Sophocles (who uses it oftenest and with the strongest effect) in *Ajax* 693ff., *Antigone* 1115ff., *Women of Trachis* 633ff., Euripides in *Heracles* 734ff. and *Electra* 859ff.

This last passage, sung by the chorus after they have been told about the death of Aigisthos, breathes the spirit of joyous dancing as they call to Electra, 'Place your foot in the dance, dear friend, leaping high to heaven, like a deer, with radiant gladness.' Antigone responds ecstatically, 'O glorious light (*phéngos*), O flashing chariot of the sun. . . .' But the most passionate expression of joy comes in *Ajax* 693ff. when the hero's loyal and affectionate followers are convinced that he does not intend to die:

> I felt a thrill of passion and I soared aloft
> With fullest joy. Oh! Oh! Come Pan, Come Pan,
> Pan! Pan! And come, thou chorus-making god,
> Apollo. Launch your dances far and wide. . . .

The opening phrase here, *éphrix' érōti*, literally 'I shuddered with *érōs*', indicates a physical reaction like an erotic orgasm, so great is the release of love and joy at the news of their master's (apparent) salvation. This, with the repetitions of the name Pan, god of wild passion, and the irregular rhythm, creates a moment of ecstatic joy unparalleled in Greek tragedy.

Besides dancing, the chief physical signs and gestures of joy in tragedy are brightness of eyes and face, tears of happiness (these two only described, on account of the masks), trembling, shouts and exclamations (which will be discussed in chapter 5), clapping hands or raised arms. (Is Helen deliberately exaggerating when she sings that her hair stood on end for joy at being restored to Menelaos in *Helen* 632–3?) It is chiefly felt in the heart (e.g. Euripides, *Electra* 402–3) or in the *phrénes*. Sophocles' fragment 824 asserts that delight and grief are both rooted in the *phrénes*, 'and so one pours forth tears even at joyous things.' The evil joy of *epichairekakía* has already been noticed.

Two further emotions deserve attention. Aristotle devotes a chapter of his *Rhetoric* to *zêlos*, 'emulation', the virtuous man's version of *phthónos*. He defines it as a feeling of pain at not possessing highly valued things that others like oneself possess, such as honour, wealth and beauty. By classifying *zêlos* as a *lúpē* and recommending it as a suitable emotion for orators to exploit Aristotle seems to imply that it was a stronger emotion in Athens than it is now. A celebrated example is Themistocles' remark that the trophy of Miltiades kept him from sleeping (Plutarch, *Themistocles* 3), and Athena in *Eumenides* 866 refers to 'a terrible *érōs* of fame' among Athenians. Clytemnestra used it to persuade Agamemnon to overcome his fear of *phthónos* and to trample the fatal fabrics as will be noticed again in chapter 9, and Odysseus hints at it when coaxing the same honour-loving king to allow the burial of Ajax (1369). It verges on 'ambition' but generally has not the unfavourable implications of that term, but Jocasta describes *philotimía* as 'worst of daimons' in *Phoenician Women* 531–2. *Zêlos* and its cognates are commoner in Sophocles and Euripides than in Aeschylus, and it sometimes approximates to a mild form of *phthónos* there.

Enthousiasmós has been noticed in the previous chapter as a mood closely associated with orgiastic cults and liable to develop among theatrical audiences, and even solitary readers, at times. It was especially potent among people joined together in a *thíasos*. When a *thíasos* became highly excited it turned into a *hesmós*, a 'swarm', like bees. (The basic meaning of *Schwärmerei* contains the same notion.) As one would expect in a Dionysiac play, the chorus in *Bacchai* shows this 'swarming' or 'teeming' mood, though the word *hesmós* is applied there only to copious outpourings of milk (710). In a remarkable phrase in the same play we are told that when the maenads were in full *enthousiasmós* 'the whole mountain and the wild animals went Bacchic with them, and nothing was left unmoved by their racing rush' (726–7).

Sophocles does not use *hesmós*, but he talks of a swarm (*smênos*) of ghosts in Fragment 795. Aeschylus uses *hesmós* four times in *Suppliant Women* (if some emendations are correct) where the chorus is in a panic at the approach of their would-be ravishers: first with reference to the 'male-filled, Egyptian-born, hybristic' crowd of their pursuers (30–1), then to a flock of frightened doves (223), then to a 'swarm' of diseases (684) and finally to an extra chorus of women more favourable to Aphrodite and Pothos (1034). As suggested in the previous chapter, there were reasons why Athenian audiences might be infected with 'swarm-feeling' more easily than a modern theatrical audience.

Of all the emotions described in the previous paragraphs the strongest and most visceral are terror, anger, passionate desire, hate and grief. Terror and grief are mainly passive and self-centred, the others are dynamic and extrovert. Grief is the least dynamic and most introverted of all, tending, as it does, to inhibit external action. On the other hand its symptoms and gestures in tragedy can be as violent as any. Some of the other feelings mentioned tend to become sentiments or mental conditions rather than emotions when they occur in their quieter forms – *philanthrōpía*, *storgḗ*, *philía*, *epichairekakía*, *póthos*, *tarachḗ*, and *zêlos*. But Phaidra's *póthos* is clearly stronger than a mere sentiment or wish, and the *storgḗ* of Alcestis is in her heart rather than in her mind. The fact that her yearning is a consequence of her *érōs* points to another difficulty in any discussion of the emotions: they sometimes merge so fully into each other that separation is impossible – anger into hate, *érōs* into *philía*, grief into fear, envy into spite. The one indivisible element in emotionalism is the *psuchḗ*, which feels every bodily sensation and mental reaction together as one experience

45

without questioning what is physical and what intellectual (or imaginary) – and without separating grief from pain, or hate from high blood-pressure. Here the *psuché* is the measure of all things. But unfortunately for any hope of precise analysis every person's *psuché* is a quite different entity. Alcibiades and Socrates are unlikely to have responded to tragic emotionalism in the same way. And every reader of this book will think and feel differently about the emotions it describes.

Other moods appear in tragedy with varying force from time to time, but they are usually more mental than emotional. Such are: *elpís* (expectation of good or evil, and so not equivalent to 'hope'), which recurs so poignantly in that drama of shattered expectations, *Persians* (261, 265, 804, 1006, 1026), wonder, confidence, benevolence and others. These, with the many less honourable qualities described by Theophrastos in his *Characters*, belong to *êthos* rather than to *páthos*. But again it is often impossible to make a firm distinction. Confidence merges into courage, courage into boldness, boldness into arrogance, arrogance into anger. A sense of justice may boil up into *némesis*. Admiration can turn into desire, wonder into *ékplēxis*. We make things easy for ourselves by saying that there are seven colours in the rainbow, but can we truly mark a division between red, orange and yellow in it?

It remains now to offer some clarification of the different kinds of participation in emotionalism that have been involved in the previous pages. In a modern dramatic performance two kinds of people show emotions, the actors with their simulated emotions (though at times they may actually feel them personally) and the audience. In the Greek theatre the presence of a chorus complicated the emotional nexus. And in emotional terms there were two sorts of chorus, the fully involved chorus who shared the *páthē* of the actors (like the Trojan women in Euripides' two plays about the aftermath of the fall of Troy), and the more detached chorus who are spectators rather than partners in the *páthē* (like the Argive Elders in the early part of *Agamemnon* and the women of Troizen in *Hippolytos*). Sometimes, then, the audience would see the chorus as the object of their emotional reaction, sometimes as sharers with themselves in their reactions to the sufferings of the characters in the play. In the second case the chorus acted almost as an instructor, telling the audience how and when to feel various emotions. This was something that orators could not exploit, as they had no intermediary between themselves and their listeners.

This duality complicates the already complex problem of 'identification' in the theatre. Sometimes an audience might 'identify' with the actors and feel their sufferings as if they were their own, like devout Christians contemplating a picture of a cruel martyrdom. *Sumpáschō* 'suffering with', was the word for this: the same is implied in 'com-passion'. At other times the audience might share the emotional responses of the chorus, hating Pentheus with the Maenads in the first part of *Bacchai*, or pitying Cassandra with the Argive Elders in *Agamemnon*.

So we can distinguish in broad outline, three kinds of emotionalism in the theatre – that of the sufferers, that of the more detached choruses (the dramatists' 'ideal spectators') and that of the audience. Occasionally, however, a fourth kind could obtrude when the audience themselves experienced a strong personal emotion. The calamitous result of the appearance of the Erinyes in *Eumenides* was presumably caused by the audience's fear for themselves not for Orestes or for the Delphic priestess. So, too, the jubilation presumably resulting in the Parthian court when an actor substituted the head of Crassus for that of Pentheus in *Bacchai* 1168ff., as described in Plutarch's *Life of Crassus* 31. But, fortunately for playwrights, such unintended emotional effects were rare, so far as we know.

One further complication in theatrical emotionalism needs consideration – the element of self-pity. When this emerges, sufferers like Oedipus and Philoctetes become a kind of chorus in themselves, singing about their woes in lyric metres and melodies. For the audience on such occasions it was not a matter of 'There's an unfortunate human being in agony and we pity him (or her)', but 'There is a pitiful scene and we share

47

in its pitifulness.' This is the difference between being sorry (or happy) *at* someone's woe and feeling sorrow *with* someone in woe. Similarly when a chorus is lamenting the woes of the protagonists they may also be mourning for their own woes like the women lamenting Patroclos as already cited. And in the same way when an audience weeps for the children of Medea they can also be weeping for dead children of their own or for the universal sufferings of humanity.

Finally, in all discussions of the emotional reactions of Athenian audiences we should keep in mind the fact already noticed that the Athenian audiences were not homogeneous. Aristotle describes (*Rhetoric* 2, 12–17) how greatly they varied in their emotional responses according to their temperaments, habits, ages and fortunes. One group might view the sorrows of Hecuba with a feeling of detached pity. Another might feel compassionate pity in the full sense of *éleos*. A third might 'identify' so fully with her that their grief would be almost as passionate as hers. But at the climaxes of great performances all constituents of the audience together with the actors and choruses could be merged by *enthousiasmós* and *Schwärmerei* into a single *thíasos* of surging emotion either of joy, as at the end of the *Oresteia*, or – as much more often – of sorrow as at the end of *Bacchai*. Some in an audience, like Plato and Augustine as quoted in chapter 1, might feel ashamed of themselves afterwards and then proceed to denounce drama. But others like Aristotle and Julian saw that such moments of self-abandonment, *ékstasis*, were beneficial as well as enjoyable.

CHAPTER FOUR

The aural element I: song, music, noises, cries and silences

The previous chapters considered the nature and effects of emotionalism in Greek tragedy. What follows now is mainly concerned with how the tragedians worked on the emotions of their audiences by skilful use of oral and visual techniques. In other words we move from the emotional to the emotive – or, in Marshall McLuhan's terms, from the message to the media. Ultimately these two are indivisible, like the mental and bodily processes in the *psuchē*. But for analytical purposes a distinction between them may be useful even though artificial.

The Athenian dramatists inherited a tradition in which poetry and music were closely allied, as the original word for poetry, *aoidē*, literally 'song,' implied. Both genres were included in the term *mousikē*, for both were believed to be inspired by Muses. The name of the tragic Muse, Melpomene, indicates singing rather than speaking. Her name, like the cognate word *molpē*, for which there is no single English equivalent, comprises both singing and dancing. This combination of words, music and dance, can provide the fullest physical expression of emotion, especially of joy, among all the arts. A trace of it survives in the phrase 'You needn't make a song and dance about it.' It may be only convention and training that prevents some singers from dancing for joy when they sing Handel's Hallelujah Chorus, and it was probably not just reverence that brought King George II and the audience to their feet when they first heard it. *Molpē* provides the last word for the joyous ending of the *Oresteia*.

Amid all the uncertainty that invests our knowledge of Greek music one fact stands out clearly: from the earliest recorded time the Greeks believed that music, usually in the form of song, had strong ethical and emotional power. The myth and cult of Orpheus attest it, and the Homeric poems exemplify it. In the *Odyssey* Odysseus is moved to tears by the song of the Phaeacian bard. In the *Iliad* Achilles soothes his angry heart by singing songs about earlier heroes. Hesiod in *Theogony* 98–103 says that the singing of songs makes a man forget his griefs and cares. (Here, as has been often noticed, we have a premonition of the doctrine of catharsis.) Some of the words used in early times to describe the power of music imply a magical process, a spell or an incantation. The myth of the Sirens emblemizes this belief, and Aeschylus exploits it in the invocation of the ghost of Darius in *Persians* and in the Binding Song of the Erinyes in *Eumenides*.

More rational attitudes emerged when music began to be studied scientifically and mathematically from the time of the Pythagoreans onwards. Still, with only one known exception – a sophist probably of the early fourth century BC, cited in the Hibeh Papyrus 13 – no rhetoricians or moralists, until the Epicureans, denied the emotional and ethical effects of music. Theophrastos, Aristotle's nephew, explained them on the grounds that both music and the emotions were the result of movements, music being caused by physical vibrations, emotion by vibrations in the *psuchē*. They also believed that the main sources of music were grief, joy and *enthousiasmós* (Plutarch, *Moralia* 623A).

More specifically, both Aristotle and Plato agreed that the various musical modes had different effects, the Dorian inducing courage and manliness, the Phrygian excitement and 'ecstasy', the Lydian relaxation and conviviality, and so on with subtle variations. These modes and their mixed or modified varieties – such as the passionately sad Mixolydian, the majestic and steady Hypodorian, and the ecstatic Hypo-phrygian – could be played in three different forms, the diatonic using intervals of a full tone, the chromatic using half-tones, and the enharmonic using still smaller intervals. These variations in turn were thought to affect the emotional force of the modes, making them more austere or more plaintive or more exciting. Plato (*Republic* 398E–399A) banned the more mournful and more convivial varieties, preferring the Dorian and the Phrygian. The latter choice surprised Aristotle, since the Phrygian mode was 'orgiastic' and 'passionate' (*Politics* 1342a 33ff.).

'Aristotle' (*Problems* 19, 48) states that the Hypodorian and Hypophrygian modes were unsuitable for the chorus. He explains this principle on the grounds that the first of these modes implies energetic action and the second grandeur and stability, qualities foreign to choruses but normal for actors. Quieter and more tearful modes suited choruses better. According to 'Plutarch' (*Moralia* 1136C–E), Aristoxenos, Aristotle's pupil, believed that Sappho invented the emotional Mixolydian type and that the tragedians took it from her and used it with the Dorian. By doing this they extended the emotional gamut of their music from heroic nobility and masculine strength (in the Dorian) to passionate feeling and feminine tenderness (in the Mixolydian). Aristoxenos is also the source of a statement in the anonymous *Life* of Sophocles (23) that Sophocles introduced the Phrygian mode into tragedy. And according to Psellos, *On Tragedy* 5, Sophocles also brought in the Lydian mode. This implies a further widening of the range of emotionalism in the tragic choruses. But unfortunately all this is a matter of theory alone, not of definitely ascertainable musical tonality.

To move on to instrumental music: the usual instrument for accompanying the choric songs and dances, the *aulós*, a pipe played like an oboe, was considered the most 'orgiastic' of all instruments (Aristotle, *Politics* 1341a 22–4, 'Longinus' 39, 2). The Bacchic and Corybantic dances were performed to its music. Plato objected to it in *Republic* 399D on the grounds that its multiplicity of notes could cause confusion in the *psuché*. Dio Chrysostom (1, 1–2) describes how, when Timotheos the pipe-player played the Orthian tune to Alexander the Great, the King leaped up to seize his arms 'like people possessed by the god' (cf. Plutarch, *Moralia* 335A). The chorus in *Women of Trachis* (217) apostrophize the pipe as

'Tyrant of my heart'. There was a specially deep-toned type of *aulós*, onomatopoeically called *bómbux* (cf. Aeschylus, Fragment 57), which Pollux describes as 'god-possessed, mad, and most suitable for orgiastic feelings'. Plutarch (*Moralia* 713A–B) says that the pipe can both soothe and excite: but when played emotionally and wildly with a multiplicity of low-register notes it can 'excite and derange a mind that is already easily moved as the result of drink'.

Two other intruments were used. The lyre, associated primarily with heroic poetry and hymns to the gods, does not play an important part in extant tragedy. Percussion instruments in the form of hand-drums or tambourines (as in the chorus in *Bacchai* 124ff.), being able to affect the pulse with their strong rhythms, can be powerfully emotive, as may be witnessed today at African dances or when the Orange drummers parade on the anniversary of the Battle of the Boyne. A production of Eugene O'Neill's adaptation of the *Oresteia*, *Mourning Becomes Electra*, in London some years ago used background drumming with tremendous emotional effect.

The thrilling sound of the trumpet, so frequent in Shakespeare's historical plays, was probably heard when it was mentioned in *Eumenides* 568 and in a fragment of the minor tragedian Achaios (37 Snell). In *Persians* 395 Aeschylus coins a vivid synaesthetic metaphor to express its brilliance –

A trumpet-call set everywhere ablaze with sound,

and Athene's voice is compared in *Ajax* 17 to a bronze Etruscan trumpet. The *Life of Aeschylus* (14) says that he made special use of trumpets.

The second way in which music can arouse emotion is by association. Different feelings would be evoked by tunes connected with, for example, erotic, or patriotic, or heroic themes and events. For instance, if a dramatist wished to evoke poignant memories from the political past of Athens he could introduce a tune from the popular Attic drinking songs (*skólia*) that went back to the time of tyranny under the Peisistratids, such as 'I'll wreathe my sword in myrtle leaves' (in memory of Harmodios and Aristogeiton) or 'Woe, woe for Leipsydrion, betrayer of comrades' (referring to an unsuccessful Alcmaeonid rising). In this way Tchaikovsky introduced the Russian national anthem in his 1812 Overture, but quite overtly and not subtly.

There is no evidence that in fact the Athenian tragedians used echoes of that kind. But they exploited similar echoes in their rhythms, as will be noticed later. If we knew as much about their music as about their rhythms we might well find, for example, that during a chorus describing feminine passion Sappho's Mixolydian was introduced as background music.

When the early Italian composers of opera were trying to reproduce the techniques of ancient drama the dominance of the musical element was fatal to their aim. The words became obscured, and the action delayed. In the best period of the Athenian drama the words were supreme, though towards the end of the fifth century Euripides was accused of distorting the normal pronunciation of words to fit a new and elaborate style of music. The chorus sang in unison, and only one instrument accompanied them, not the thunderous orchestra of our opera. The relationship between the tonality of the words (as indicated by the tonic accents), the melody that they sang, and the melody played on the pipe, is much disputed. On the analogy of ancient Sanskrit and modern Chinese song it seems likely that the natural tonality of the words was to some degree preserved, and the evidence of the few surviving fragments of Greek choral music seem to support this. 'Plutarch' (*Moralia* 1141B) says that the instrumental music was in unison with the voice until a musician called Krexos introduced heterophonic and pararhythmic accompaniments, probably in the late fifth or early fourth century. The divorce of words and music probably helped to cause the decline of choruses in later drama.

The contrast between the melodies of Greek tragedy and the elaborate harmonies of modern music is like the contrast between the simplicity of the ancient stage-settings and the elaboration of theatrical scenery today. And it accords with

53

Pericles' memorable words in his Funeral Speech (Thucydides 2, 40, 1) about the Athenians, 'We are lovers of the beautiful without extravagance.' On the other hand, the resources of the melodies of the Greek modes with their various modifications and 'colours' were far from simple. As a contemporary expert has observed, 'A Greek composer had a great wealth of subtle intonations at his disposal, and . . . Greek melodies must have had a delicacy and firmness of outline to which the melodies of modern music can offer no parallel.' Whether this melodic style evoked a stronger emotional response than the rich harmonies of a modern orchestra is an open question. Arguably the more complex forms dilute rather than intensify emotionalism.

'Now that the genius of music has fled from tragedy, tragedy is, strictly speaking dead.' So Nietzsche affirmed in his *Birth of Tragedy*. Contemporary directors of films have learned to use emotive music as a background for their most emotional scenes. Here the music is an *obbligato* to the action, and not to the dancing and singing as in Greek tragedy. But its use may be one of the reasons why audiences tend to be more emotional in our cinemas than in our theatres. An experience told to the present writer tends to confirm this. While someone was watching, with growing excitement, a tense moment in an amateur film, suddenly the background music faded out. Immediately his emotional temperature dropped. The visual dimension by itself was not enough to sustain the emotional climax.

Even when films had to be silent the need for music was recognized by providing a pianist to play suitable accompaniments. Here, too, lapses could occur. One musician, it is said, disliked playing 'programme music', preferring to play finer, but irrelevant, pieces by his favourite Bach and Chopin. The manager told him that he must make the music support the action. The musician tried to conform but kept wandering back into classical pieces. One day while paying more attention to his music than to the film he suddenly remembered his instructions. Glancing up at the screen he saw what looked like a dinner-party in ancient times. He began to play 'For he's a jolly good fellow' to suggest a convivial mood. Too late he realized that the scene was the Last Supper. It would be possible for composers of music for drama to deliberately exploit dissonances of that kind either satirically or to cause emotional confusion in the listeners. But without further knowledge of Greek music one cannot say whether this was ever practised.

Music's ugly sister, noise, can be highly emotive in a more primitive way. (The third, and most intelligent sister of the sonic family, speech, will be introduced in the next chapter.) Dramatic noise can take several forms. It can be human or non-human. It can be either the cause or the result of emotion – that is to say, emotive or emotional. It can be described or actually produced. It is especially potent as a cause of fear. Theophrastos asserted (Plutarch, *Moralia* 38A) that no sensation of sight, taste or touch could cause such 'ecstasies, flutterings and confusions of the *psuché*' as 'noise, hubbub and resonant sounds'. Zeno believed (Diogenes Laertius, *Lives of Philosophers* 7, 113) that it specially caused panic fear.

The best example in Greek tragedy of the use of non-human noise to create an atmosphere of near-panic is in *Seven against Thebes*. References to various noises in the background, mostly from the attacking enemy, reverberate right through the play – noises from arms and armour, from horses and chariots and harness, from thrown stones, from shouting warriors, from frightened women and children in the city, from a trumpet-call and (in imagery) from a wave of the sea and a snake. These are all described noises. Mixed through them are the actual noises made by the chorus of frightened women, consisting of many exclamations and of onomatopoeic words like *pátagos*, *ótobos*, *ktúpos*, *kónabos*, which embody the sounds that are being described. To give extra vividness to the chorus's terror at the noise, Aeschylus introduces a synaesthetic metaphor, similar to that quoted above for a trumpet-call, 'I see the din' (*ktúpon dédorka*) meaning that their sensation of hearing is as sharp and distinct as if they could see

55

the sound. Altogether there are over fifty references to noise of one kind or another in the play. There is nothing like this sustained emphasis on frightening noise in any other Greek tragedy.

In a modern theatre mechanical means would usually be employed to give background support to the kind of noises described in *Seven*. Such support, like elaborate scenery, was neither needed nor, so far as we know, enlisted in the Greek theatre – with one possible exception. When the awe-inspiring sound of thunder was mentioned in *Prometheus* 1044–5, 1082–3, and *Oedipus at Colonos* 1456 and 1514, perhaps the 'thunder-maker' (*bronteîon*) was used, but it may have been introduced (like the 'lightning-maker', *keraunoskopeîon*) at a later date. Anyway, the performances did not need any such noises-off. Descriptions accompanied by appropriate physical reactions would suffice.

But the prevailing noises of tragedy were naturally of human origin. Every play has its nexus of inarticulate sounds of grief or fear or joy or triumph and other emotions – sobs, groans, screams, gasps, laughs and ululations. (Ancient Greek offers no special term for a sigh: but in any case sighs would have been inaudible in most of a Greek theatre.) Onomatopoeic words are frequent in descriptions of these vocal gestures. We find *góos* for a resonant sound of grief, *kōkutós* or *iugmós* for a shrill wail, *kraugḗ* for a harsh scream. Some terms could be used either for grief or joy, like the ritual *ololugḗ* of women and the *alalagḗ* of men. Then there are the many interjections that will be discussed later.

The most bizarre human noises in all Greek tragedy are those made by the Erinyes in the opening scene of *Eumenides*. First the Pythian priestess describes them as snorting (*rhénkousi*, from *rhúnchos* 'a snout'). Though onomatopoeically this word could stand for either a snort or a snore, it must mean a snort here because the priestess adds 'with repellent puffs of breath'. Later in the scene their noise moves from description to actuality. A stage direction states that they are to utter a mewing or moaning sound (*mugmós*, cf. *muchmós* in *Odyssey*

24, 416), then an *o*-sound (*ōgmós*), followed by a shriller repeated *mugmós*. Next, when they begin to dream of hunting their prey, the sound they make is described as being like the clangorous baying of hounds (*klangaíneis*, 131, also used of a dragon or snake in *Seven* 381, and cf. in *Agamemnon* 156). All this monstrous cacophony must have contributed strongly to the panic in the audience.

In *Prometheus* 355 we are told that the dreadful sound coming from the hideous jaws of the monster Typhon was a hiss or whistle (*surízōn*, another onomatopoeic word, the *z* being pronounced as *sd*), and so, too, the noise made by the nosebands of the horses in *Seven* 463. (Dramatists had reason to dislike that word, as it was also used for the hiss of hostile spectators.) Sophocles and Euripides prefer to express noises in terms of imagery as in *Ajax* 321–2 and *Heracles* 869–70, where the sounds made by the heroes are compared to a bull's bellowings.

In contrast with these inarticulate sub-human noises, the most frequent and most expressive noises of Greek tragedy are articulate though not quite verbal in the sense that they are not generally subject to rules of syntax, they do not belong to the categories of noun, verb, etc., they are not declined or conjugated, and they have no descriptive force. These are the utterances usually described as interjections or ejaculations (*epiphonēmata*). They are the most primitive of all human sounds, more like animal cries than speech. They are of supreme importance for the emotional effects of Greek tragedy, setting up physical and emotional vibrations that no articulate words could. Yet editors often ignore them, and translators are commonly satisfied with a perfunctory 'Oh', 'Ah' or 'Alas'.

Compared to English, ancient Greek had an extraordinarily wide selection of those emotional cries, over thirty of them. Most of them consist of vowels alone – *a, ai, e, ea, eē, euoi, ē, ēe, eia, iai, ieu, iou, iō, iōa, oa, oi, ō, ōē*, and possibly *iauoi* (see *Frogs* 1029). (Accents vary, and perhaps the normal accentuation marks would be misleading here.) Many of these are repeated several times in succession for emphasis. Some of them may have been uttered with an intake of breath, for example *ea* which often seems to indicate a gasp of surprise.

Others contained a consonantal element – *attatai, apappai, da, eleleu, ioph, om*. (The last two, from Aeschylus, *Suppliant Women* 825–9, may be ghost words in a corrupted text, but the scene there is extremely emotional.) Others containing consonants are *mu, ototoi, papai, popax, popoi, pheu*. Two of these were sometimes reduplicated. *Ototoi* is variously extended, reaching its maximum in Hecuba's heart-broken cry when she sees the flames blaze up from burning Troy – *ottototototoi*. Most sensational of all are Philoctetes' agonized screams (745–6 and 754): *papai, apappapai, papappapappapappapai* (but the text for obvious reasons varies). This extraordinary outcry – in which, as Jebb notes, the recurrent *pi* may indicate trembling lips – is the culmination of an elaborate crescendo and diminuendo of exclamations. As Philoctetes begins to feel the pain from his poisoned foot he cries *a* four times (732) and later again four times (739). Then, when the full spasm of agony seizes him, he cries the full *papai* sequence as given above. After it he speaks rationally for a while. But, as another spasm seizes him he cries in succession (784–96) *papai, pheu, papai, oimoi, attatai, pheu, papai, papai, ōmoi*, at intervals until the pain subsides. But gradually as his mind turns to cursing his enemies, his physical agony is absorbed in his feelings of hatred and self-pity. (One is reminded of Blaise Pascal's curing of a toothache by concentrating on a mathematical problem.)

Even Oedipus after he has blinded himself does not utter such a terrible cry as Philoctetes, but only *aiai, pheu, iō, oimoi*, in various repetitions. The reason is presumably because some time has elapsed since Oedipus blinded himself, while Philoctetes is actually feeling the full stab of pain. In *Women of Trachis* 1004ff. when the poison eats into Heracles' flesh, he, most enduring of heroes, cries *ee, totoi, pheu, e, e and iō*. In *Heracles* 1140ff., where his pain is emotional not physical, his exclamations are quieter.

It is impossible to confine many of these exclamations to single emotions. Much depends on the emotional situation and on the way in which actors or chorus pronounced the various syllables. *Papai* and *popoi* can express surprise or anger as well as pain. (Cassandra in *Agamemnon* 1072–1114 first cries *popoi* three times and then changes to *papai* when her vision becomes sharper.) *Ototoi* and its variants generally indicate grief more than pain, but often the two are inseparable. *Pheu* – pronounced with a strong *p* sound, not as *f* – expresses sorrow, anger, astonishment, admiration, disgust, or mixtures of these. Cassandra's double *pheu* when she smells the 'blood-dripping' slaughter inside the palace (1307) is like our 'Ugh!' or Hamlet's 'Pah!' as he handles the malodorous skull of Yorick – indeed *pheu* could sound like a combination of the two. Simple *a* can express pity, envy, contempt, warning, reproof, or loss of patience. In *Women of Trachis* 220 and *Ajax* 694 *io* expresses joy, but elsewhere usually grief or suffering. The Bacchic *euoi* voices the height of ecstatic joyousness in *Bacchai* 141, and elsewhere. Sometimes the exclamations are part of a metrical line, sometimes they stand by themselves *extra metrum*. In the second case we may perhaps presume that they are drawn out longer perhaps even to the length of a full line.

A noteworthy example of how the Greek analytical mind can intrude at times into a highly emotional scene – with almost ludicrous effects to our ears – is in *Persians* 1031–3. Xerxes has just told the chorus how he tore his clothes in grief at the disaster. The chorus exclaim *papai, papai*. 'No', cries Xerxes, 'Even more than *papai*.' 'Yes', the chorus reply, 'Even twice and three times.' The play ends in a climax of reduplicated cries (with particles to emphasize them) – *oioi, oioi . . . iō iō . . . iōa* indeed . . . *iōa* certainly, yes, yes, . . . *iō, iō . . . eeee . . . eeee*. It looks absurd on paper, almost like the bird-songs in Aristophanes' *Birds*. But, at the end of a play in which the dreaded enemies of the Athenians lamented their defeat, the audience were likely to have been deeply moved by a mixture of pity – or at least *philanthrōpía* – for the Persians and joy for themselves, and perhaps even by a touch of *epichairekakía*.

When these various cries were uttered by uninhibited actors in full voice – more tolerable in an unroofed theatre – they must have had a tremendous emotional effect. For us it needs a great effort to feel anything like it. The weight of tradition in northern Europe and America is against such open-mouthed and open-hearted demonstrations of grief, pain and joy, in life or in literature. And, so far as translation is concerned, we have not the vocabulary to produce equivalents for the many Greek forms. Perhaps it would usually be best to insert instead a stage direction like 'She screams with pain' or 'They groan in grief', but that loses the essential vocalic qualities that will be discussed in the next chapter – for example, the labial consonants and open vowels of Philoctetes' long scream, or the staccato effect of a prolonged *ototoi*. The only way to appreciate their full power is to utter them oneself or to hear someone else utter them with full force and in the spirit of the context.

In the most lamentatory passages of Greek tragedy exclamations are exploited to a degree far beyond anything in modern drama. As has been emphasized in recent studies, the fact that the ancient Greeks were accustomed to ritual lamentations in their public and private life made this more tolerable. (Lucian's essay *On Grief* stigmatizes excessive public mourning in his day.) In Ireland similar ritual lamentations survived in rural areas until recently (as in modern Greece and Yugoslavia). Consequently a near parallel in modern drama to the lamentations of Athenian drama is provided by the scene in Synge's *Riders to the Sea* when the mourning women raise the *caoin* ('keen') over the corpse of a drowned fisherman. But Synge, unlike his Greek predecessors, did not give us the benefit of being able to read a transcription of these lamentations in his play. Instead he offered only two stage directions, 'The women are keening softly and swaying themselves with a slow movement', and 'The keen rises a little more loudly from the women and then sinks away.' There are no such directions in Greek tragedy apart from the exception in *Eumenides* mentioned earlier. But how much more potent are the written records of the various emotional cries that we have in the Greek texts! To ignore their intense emotionalism as one reads a Greek tragedy is like crossing the Sahara in an air-conditioned car.

Silence can be as expressive as noise or speech, especially among people so talkative as the Greeks – silence in the course of the action or described silence. In the action, the longer the silence the greater its emotional power. Long silences are exemplified in the pathetic silence of Cassandra in *Agamemnon* 783–1071, in the tortured, tense silence of Prometheus for the first eighty-seven lines of his tragedy, in the defiant silence of Antigone (*Antigone* 384–440), in the ashamed silence of Phaidra (as implied in *Hippolytos* 297), in the desolate silence of Heracles after realizing that he has killed his children (*Heracles* 1178–1230), and (in two lost plays by Aeschylus) in Niobe's heart-broken silence and Achilles' wrathful silence (mocked by Euripides in *Frogs* 911–13 – 'not a grunt out of them'). Possibly, too – but this is much disputed – Clytemnestra is silently present when the chorus in *Agamemnon* 83–7 ask the reason for the joyful illuminations. (Such a refusal to answer a direct question without an obvious reason is unparalleled, but we must remember that Clytemnestra is a woman *sans pareil*. After the Watchman's ominous remark about her masterful character, and his hints about alarming conditions inside the palace, a proud, silent entry and exit would be distinctly sinister.)

Silence is especially noticeable at the end of a character's appearance on the scene as well as at the beginning, witness the desperate silent exits of Jocasta, Eurydice and Deianeira. Agamemnon is silent as he walks over the blood-coloured fabrics to his doom, while in contrast the Queen disguises her nervous excitement with a flood of almost incoherent speech. There are also the brief silences in the middle of dialogues, indicated by broken syntax. These will be considered in chapter 8.

These are silences in action. There are also many effective described silences. One of the most pathetic occurs when the chorus in *Agamemnon* 412–13 picture the effect on Menelaos of Helen's departure: 'There he is, silent, dishonoured,

unreviling . . ., yearning for her who is across the sea. . . .'
Euripides exploits a different kind of stillness in *Bacchai*
1084–5. Just before the ghastly scene when the maenads tear
Pentheus asunder the Messenger says

> The air fell silent, and the wooded glade
> Kept its leaves still. No sound of wild beasts' cries.

(This motif of an ominous calm before an epiphany of super-
natural beings goes back to *Odyssey* 12, 168–9, where there is a
sudden windless calm before Odysseus reaches the dread
Sirens.) Similarly the chorus in *Agamemnon* (737–40) briefly
describes a 'spirit of windless calm' before disaster swooped
down on Troy. But no tragedian uses the theme better than
Euripides in *Bacchai*, where one can imagine the quiet note of
menace in the Messenger's voice.

CHAPTER FIVE

The aural element II:
the music of the spoken word

Attention in this chapter will continue to be given to emotional and emotive acoustic elements in the performances of Greek tragedy. But in contrast with the last chapter, which considered non-semantic sounds, the subject here will be articulate sounds – words in their oral and aural aspects. To some extent it is misleading to treat words in terms of their euphonic qualities alone. Except in nonsense-writing their sounds and their meanings are always interlocked. But if one always keeps that inter-relation in mind it may be helpful to consider the sound-aspects in isolation for a while, just as metrists study metre mostly without immediate reference to the meaning of the passages they are scanning, and anatomists study body-structure without regard to the personality inside the rib-cage.

Classical writers recognized that speech, especially when pronounced in the resonant and rhythmical way that orators and actors used, had all the properties of song, though to a less perceptible degree. Both were regarded as forms of *mousikē*, and both were produced by the same instrument. In teaching poetry at present most of the emphasis is placed on the semantic force of the words – what they state and what they describe or symbolize – and the musical element is often neglected. Much of modern poetry itself is intellectual rather than sensuous, and musicality is neglected or even, since Swinburne's sonic excesses, despised by many poets. But Greek poetry retained its musical qualities until the end of the pagan period, and the Greek critics continued to notice and admire them.

One of the chief reasons for this was the fact that Greek poetry was composed essentially for hearing rather than for silent reading. In dramatic poetry the classical dramatists, being in direct control of the production, could, and no doubt would, insist that their actors and choruses should take due care with the musical qualities of their words. As producers the tragedians could curb the inclinations of actors to reduce the speeches and dialogues to ordinary conversational levels, and they could ensure that every rhythm and cadence would be faithfully rendered.

The normal word for the poet's preparation of his cast for performance, *didáskein*, meant 'to teach'. No description of how the Greek dramatists went about this task has survived. Perhaps we can see something like their methods in an account of how a modern poet behaved in similar circumstances. When W. B. Yeats was training a reader to record some of his poems for broadcasting he first told him to avoid histrionics. The sensuous and passionate qualities of the poem should dominate, not the style and mannerisms of an actor. (In antiquity the equivalent of this would be advice not to speak the speeches like an orator.) Yeats spent much time in bringing out the affective and mimetic elements in the poems to be read. He prescribed a 'defiant rhythm' in the phrase 'a tattered coat upon a stick' to emphasize 'bitterness against old age'. He showed how to put a 'skipping rhythm' into the phrase 'to where the cricket sings' by shortening the syllables in 'cricket' and by making a short break before and after it. He insisted that if there was to be a musical accompaniment it should be composed so that no word would be given an intonation or an accentuation that it would not have in speech. He himself, like Tennyson, spoke his poems in a resonant, incantatory tone of voice, and he constantly emphasized the incantatory power of poetry.

Yeats was 'teaching' short lyric poems. A Greek poet-dramatist with a tetralogy of over 4,000 lines on his hands had no time for such details. But as a poet his overall aim would have been much the same, to make the sensuous and emotive qualities of his words as effective as possible rather than – as many modern producers of Shakespeare do – to emphasize the conceptual meaning at the expense of the poetry. Ultimately the physical material of poetry, as of music, is vibrations in the air – vibrations which of themselves can, like music, affect our emotions and charm our ears. So if we wish to find a modern analogue for the Greek poet-dramatist-producer it would be well to think more in terms of a musical composer-conductor rather than of an independent producer acting as a middle-man between the author and the actors.

There are six phonetic elements in speech that a poet can exploit for emotional affect. Three are indicated in the Greek texts as we have them – rhythm, timbre-quality (the phonetic differences between dentals, labials, closed and open vowels, and so on), and pitch-variation (as indicated by the Greek accent-marks). The other three – volume, speed and voice-quality – are not deducible from the alphabetic signs. For them one has to rely on stage-directions (very rare in our texts) or statements in the plays.

The emotional effects of rhythm were a subject of intensive study in Greece since the fifth century. Thrasymachos, the early expert in appeals for pity, was particularly interested in them. Subsequently moralists, like Plato, as well as rhetoricians continued to examine their ethical qualities. But in the later period Greek scholars began to treat metrics as a theoretical discipline almost like pure mathematics. Modern metricians have generally followed this structural approach and have tended to deprecate theories that particular metres are intended to have, or can have, specific psychological effects. In the following paragraphs the older attitude will be adopted, together with the convention that all syllables are either long or short (or: heavy or light). In actual speech, of course, there is an immense variety of syllable-quantities, as some ancient metricians recognized. But until a scholar devises a better system of metrical analysis one must use the old method. One other controversial matter cannot be pursued here. Was there stress as well as quantity in the rhythms of Greek poetry? The evidence is inadequate for a clear conclusion. On the one hand classical writers do not definitely refer to it; on the other, it seems linguistically probable that the tonic accent involved some degree of stress just as the stress accent in modern Greek usually involves some elevation of pitch.

Rhythm, like melody, can be emotionally effective in two ways – by direct action and by association. Obvious examples of direct effects are to be seen in the use of successive long syllables to express caution, calmness or melancholy, and successive short syllables for eagerness, agitation and excitement (cf. Plutarch, *Moralia* 747D). There are no less than nineteen short syllables in succession at a tragic moment in *Heracles* (1061–2). The excited short syllables of Agave and the chorus in *Bacchai* 1169–99 contrast with the spondees of the beginning of the pitiful scene in 1200–1, and there is a similar contrast in the earthquake scene in 578–603. Changes from lyric metres to iambic trimeters are also involved there, as also when Clytemnestra's slow trimeters (with a high proportion of spondees), in which she resolutely proclaims her murder of Agamemnon, are followed by a series of eleven short, and only two long, syllables from the appalled chorus (*Agamemnon* 1407–8). Clytemnestra continues to speak in calm trimeters against the chorus's lyric metres until 1462. A change from iambic trimeters to trochaic catalectic tetrameters generally shows an increase in emotional excitement (e.g. *Agamemnon* 1649ff., *Heracles* 855ff., *Phoenician Women* 588ff.), while a change from lyric metres to trochaic tetrameters can show a decrease in emotionalism (e.g. *Bacchai* 604ff.). The iambic trimeter itself could be made more excited by increasing the number of resolutions, as in *King Oedipus* 825–7.

Besides acting as supplementary expressions of emotion, rhythms could also directly affect the feelings of a listening audience. The Greek psychologists explained the emotive qualities of rhythm in the same way as they explained those of music: the emotions being movements in the *psuchē* are sympathetically affected by the vibrations of sounds. Rhythm could have a stronger effect than melody, since the heart-beat is essentially rhythmical. The Greek physicians Herophilos and Galen compared the rhythm of the heart, with its systole and diastole, to that of a metrical foot (Galen 9, 463–4 Kühn). They were speaking of the regular pulse. But one can extend the analogy. The dochmiac rhythm that occurs at most of the major climaxes resembles the irregular heart-beats of a highly excited person. Its structure varies from a jerky alternation of longs and shorts to a gabble of short syllables whose metre can only be deduced from the proximity of more regular lines. In prolonged sequence dochmiacs could affect listeners like a drum-beat varying, in terms of our stress-rhythm, from tat-tát-tát-tat-tát-to-tat-tat tat-tat-tat-tat-tát.

Rhythms can also be emotive through association, as has been exemplified for melody. When Aeschylus wanted to give to some lines of the chorus in *Agamemnon* 122ff. both a heroic and an oracular tone he used dactylic hexameters. Similarly Sophocles recalled the heroic status of sick Philoctetes by making Neoptolemos use hexameters in 839–42. When Aeschylus wanted to create an amorous aura for a moment in a description of Helen's departure for Troy (*Agamemnon* 690–2) he employed a lyric rhythm which the Athenians would readily recognize, that of Anacreon's love-poetry. Similarly when Euripides adopted ionic rhythms for the opening chorus of the *Bacchai* he probably intended to underline the Asian origin and the orgiastic mood of the Maenads.

A reservation must be made here. Many modern metrists reject belief in significant rhythm of this kind. But is it likely that a rhythm-loving people like the early Athenians would not be sensitive to such nuances? To take a modern parallel: suppose that a President of the United States at some ceremony connected with the memory of Abraham Lincoln were to say 'confident *from* his courage, *through* his courage, and *with* his courage', would any educated hearer fail to recognize the rhythmical allusion to Lincoln's famous 'government of the people, by the people and for the people' even though no two words are the same? Or again, can anyone brought up in the same religious tradition as A. E. Housman miss the rhythmical echoes of evangelical hymns in his poems – ironical echoes, indeed, in view of the bleak agnosticism of Housman's beliefs.

Parodists frequently use deliberate clashes between metrical memories and new words. James Joyce in *Finnegans Wake* offers many examples of this device. In recent times the most celebrated use of a rhythmical motif was when the tat-tat-tat-tát of the opening bar of Beethoven's Fifth Symphony became a symbol of resistance and victory during the war of 1939–45 – and very aptly so to the Hellenic ear since it is the equivalent of a fourth paeon in Greek metrical terms, and the paeon was traditionally the rhythm of victory and joy.

One must enter a *caveat* at this point. It is not being asserted that the use in tragedy of rhythms like hexameters and anacreontics and paeonics always carries clear emotional overtones. In fact they are sometimes used when any such associations are hard to perceive. What is being suggested is that the tragedians did use these metrical modes at times, when the context demanded, to reinforce emotionalism. This is what happens in life. At solemn or critical moments we use words and listen to words more sensitively than in normal conditions. It is the same, too, with the poetic use of onomatopoeia. A word like 'cricket' in some contexts will be merely denotative. In others it must jump like the insect, as Yeats prescribed. And these relevancies of word-music would be emphasized by the speaker or actor when required.

The second potentially emotional and emotive element in the sound of words is timbre or 'tone-colour' (*Klangfarbe*). The Greeks had a superbly phonetic alphabet with its seven distinct vowels (the differences between *epsilon* and *eta*, and *omicron* and *omega*, were qualitative as well as quantitative) and seventeen consonants. (The theory that they expanded it from the Phoenician alphabet, which had no vowel signs, for the special purpose of recording the musical sounds of poetry is not improbable.) But these written symbols remained secondary to the oral tradition in poetry until the end of the fifth century. Actors and choruses probably learned their words orally, not from written scripts, though presumably – but it is not absolutely certain – the poet-dramatist-director had a written version. The supreme value of the written text was that it preserved plays after the performances. And thanks to information provided by Greek phoneticians we can get a fair idea of what those inert black marks on white pages originally sounded like.

In the various distinct tone-colours of Greek the poets had, as it were, a whole range of instruments to call on for musical and emotional effects, like a modern composer-conductor with a symphony orchestra. Their single basic instrument, the human voice, was so versatile that it constituted a whole orchestra of wind and percussion instruments in itself (though only, of course, for melodic sequences, not for harmony). The various types of consonants provided a kind of percussion and muting. The vowels offered the equivalent of notes from oboe, flute and saxophone.

The ancient literary critics had nothing to say about the emotional and emotive uses of tone-colour, though they recognized its value for imitative onomatopoeia. A sceptic may argue that there is a simple reason for this omission: there are no intrinsically sad or fearful or joyous vowels or consonants. Clearly that is true of these sounds as separate phonetic symbols. But is it true of speech-sounds in definitely emotional contexts? The sound of *sigma* by itself is neutral. But when it recurs seven times on the lips of the furious Medea (476), its sibilance, stressed no doubt by the actor, acquires the sinister texture of a serpent's hiss. Perhaps the same implication is in the eight sigmas of Ajax's reference to the hated Atreidai (390). Another probable example occurs when the angry and scornful Oedipus denounces Teiresias in a line (*King Oedipus* 371) containing nine percussive *taus*. This is not mimetic onomato- poeia in which 'the sound echoes the sense'. It is the kind of onomatopoeia in which the sound expresses the feeling, as in our interjection written as 'tut-tut'. Sometimes both types merge, as when the Messenger in *Antigone* 1232 tells how Haimon expressed his scorn and contempt for his father by spitting at him. The Greek word is *ptúsas*. Reinforced by the strong alliteration of *p* and *pt*, in the rest of the line, it vividly embodies the feeling, action and sound of that repulsive gesture.

Expressiveness by means of tone-colour could be extremely subtle. It can only be detected by reading, or listening to someone else reading, the Greek with its full sonic values, and by ears attuned to speech-music. No doubt there is a risk of hearing mirages, so to speak, in this respect, just as writers on symbolism sometimes find implications beyond the scan of ordinary mortals. For example, to the present writer there is a feeling of sadness and strain in the recurrent *etas* and difficult vowel-sequences in the opening line of the *Iliad* in contrast with the *alphas* and smooth-running vocalism of the first line of the *Odyssey*; and then the *Odyssey's* second line with its tongue-twisting *plánchthē* introduces a feeling of stress and strain as one might expect in a reference to the hero's arduous wanderings. (There is a similarly apt set of tongue-twisters in *Prometheus* 362.)

It is hard to experience the full effects of such differences of sound-texture in a language that is no longer spoken, especially for those who, like the present writer, were accustomed for most of their lives to reading it silently. As a plainer example of its effect, one may contrast these lines of Milton's joyous *L'Allegro* and his melancholy *Il Penseroso*:

> Come, and trip it as you go,
> On the light fantastic toe,

and

> Come, pensive nun, devout and pure,
> Sober, steadfast and demure.

Though the difference is partly in the rhythm and the syntax, the timbre and the consonantal weight clearly contribute to the contrast of mood. When similar effects are alleged in Greek poetry scholars sometimes suggest that in fact the alliteration, or assonance, or sound-texture in general, is accidental. Would any musician say the same about tone-patterns in a nocturne by Chopin or a sonata by Beethoven? But convincing evidence for or against the existence of emotional qualities in the sound of Greek will not be available until the phonetic frequencies of every line in extant Greek poetry have been tabulated and analysed (as has been done for the Homeric poems, but without the tonic accents). If it then becomes clear that certain sonic patterns occur with abnormal frequency in specially emotional contexts then a fair presumption of deliberate choice will be established, and if not, not. Meanwhile one can only rely on personal impressions and on what the ancient rhetoricians and literary critics said.

Here the best support comes from Aristotle in his *Rhetoric* (1403b 27ff.), where in a very brief reference to oratorical 'delivery' (*hupócrisis* which Demosthenes considered the supreme element in effective oratory according to Cicero, *Brutus* 68), he observes that an orator who wishes to arouse emotion must know how to use rhythm, volume and voice-melody ('the sharp, low and middle tones'), for that purpose. He adds that 'those [actors] who use these properly nearly always won the prizes in the dramatic contests.' He does not mention the three other qualities under review in this chapter – timbre-quality, voice-quality, and speed (though that was probably included in rhythm). But he affirms the general principle that the sonic properties of words should be exploited to excite *páthos* in an audience.

Another possible – perhaps even probable – use of timbre-quality should also be kept in mind. Milton's *Lycidas*, that marvel of subtle speech-music, begins with the line

Yet once more, O ye laurels, and once more,

and later at the chief emotional turning-point it has

Weep no more, woeful shepherds, weep no more. . . .

The predominance of long *o*-sounds is unmistakable. They provide a bass undertone of lamentation to the conceptual meaning, as if someone were moaning 'Oh' five times in the background. The high proportion of *omegas* in *King Oedipus* 5–7 and *Ajax* 657–77 would enable an actor to achieve the same effect.

The third salient quality of speech that is recorded in our

Greek texts, pitch-variation, obviously could be a vehicle for emotionalism. In everyday speech one of the surest indications of emotional conditions is voice-melody, the falling tones of sadness, the rising tones of joy, the low tones of melancholy, the high tones of fear, the wavering tones of disturbance, the level tones of confidence. There are two ways by which a writer can prescribe the tones he wishes his readers to use. The first is obviously available to all, namely to use descriptive words like 'shrill and sharp' (*oxús*, expressing grief in *Persians* 1056, *Women of Trachis* 963, and elsewhere) or 'low and heavy' (*barús* expressing melancholy in *Persians* 572 and *Philoctetes* 208.) The second way of indicating pitch is unique to Greek among European languages, Greek with its tonic accents – acute, grave, and circumflex – showing the tone-level at which each syllable must be pronounced. In the absence of such marks readers of poetry and prose in all other European languages have no built-in guidance in the written text to tell them how to inflect their voices. If – as once actually happened – someone reading the Christmas lesson about 'tidings of great joy' drops his voice noticeably on the word 'joy' it sheds a momentary gloom over the listeners. But no one reading the original Greek (St Luke 2, 10) with the accents pronounced in the classical way could have let his voice lapse, since the rise and fall of the voice-level is prescribed by the accent-marks.

We are entering on an extremely controversial area of Greek linguistics here. It is generally agreed that the acute accent indicated a rise in tone of approximately a fifth and that the circumflex indicated a rising-falling tone round the same high level. The value of the grave is disputed. Did it indicate a modified version of the acute, or a reduction to the low level of pitch? (The evidence seems to favour the former view.) At any rate we can be sure of this: a Greek author could choose his words to some extent for their tone-values as well as for their rhythm and timbre-quality, and he could be confident that anyone reading those words aloud would use approximately the same voice-melodies (as in some oriental and African languages). Further, there is evidence from the fifth century

BC that the Athenians were sensitive to a lapse in pronunciation of the tonic accents, in the incident referred to in Aristophanes' *Frogs* 303–4, when the emotional level of a line in
Orestes sank into bathos as the result (partly at least) of the
actor's pronunciation of an acute accent as a circumflex.

Statistics again are lacking to determine whether the Greek
tragedians exploited their control of voice-melody for
emotional effect. A possible example is in the melancholy
speech of Ajax when he is trying, in vain, to reconcile himself
to dishonour. The proportion of grave accents in line 669 is
very high – that is to say the frequency of high-pitched
syllables is low – and the three circumflexes in line 677 suggest a
melancholy cadence. (One may compare Verdi's use of a
virtual monotone to express Othello's despair in *Otello* 3, 3.)
But this may be a subjective impression. What needs to be
emphasized, however, is that while a modern poet is at the
mercy of readers, actors and producers, for the intonation of
his poems, the Greek dramatists were not. If they chose the
word *nómos* the reader or actor *had* to pronounce it with the
first syllable sounding at about a fifth above the second: if they
chose *nomós*, it *had* to be the reverse. English has a built-in
stress as in the noun 'prótest' and the verb 'protést'. But stress,
being less musical than pitch-variation, is more intellectual
than emotional.

There is a different way, however, by which a poet can
choose his words to suggest levels of tone, in other European
languages besides ancient Greek. Narrow vowels are generally
pronounced at a higher pitch than broad vowels, as in the
contrast between 'trip it' and 'once more' and between *iúzō* and
oimōzō. The *upsilons* in the phrase *aútei d'oxú* in *Persians* 1058
suggest a special shrillness of tone. But perhaps the pitch-
variation in such cases was too slight to be perceptible.

The three other elements of speech as defined earlier – speed,
volume and voice-quality – can also be effective in expressing
and arousing emotion – a tense accelerando, a menacing crescendo, a growling threat. These depend largely on the speaker
rather than on the author of the words to be spoken. But to

some extent the author can control them. He can inhibit or facilitate high speed by choosing or avoiding long syllables and thick consonant-clusters, as Pope states and illustrates in his *Essay on Criticism* (370–1):

> When Ajax strives, some Rock's vast Weight to throw,
> The Line too *labours*, and the Words move slow.

Homer (as Dionysios of Halicarnassos observed, and Pope knew well) used a similar technique in describing the toil of Sisyphos in *Odyssey* 11, 593–8. Obviously, too, the poet can prescribe differences in speed by specific references in his text to quickness or slowness, and also, as already noticed, by variations in metre.

Volume is not inherent in the nature of words. The same word can be shouted or murmured, yelled or whispered, roared or muttered, though some speech-sounds are less amenable to volume-variation than others. For example, the letters *m* and *n* naturally have a muting effect, and broad vowels lend themselves to shouts better than narrow vowels. Occasionally the context indicates how loudly or softly words are spoken. The shouts of Philoctetes in his agony are indicated in 208–9, 216, 218, in contrast with Odysseus' instructions to Neoptolemos to speak quietly in 22. Polymestor, after he has been blinded, calls 'with a shout, a shout, a shout' in *Hecuba* 1091. And there are similar indications in Sophocles' *Electra* 830 and in *Prometheus* 743.

Voice-quality – huskiness, breathiness, resonance, and innumerable other variations – can to a limited extent be helped by diction. One is more or less forced to use a harsh timbre in Milton's

> Grate on their scrannel pipes of wretched straw,

such as is impossible in Virgil's warbling line,

> *Tityre, tu patulae recubans sub tegmine fago.*

Similarly, while a name like Tityros or Lalage suggests a pleasing quality of voice, Calchas with its guttural sounds suggests harsh tones (as Aeschylus indicates in *Agamemnon* 156).

Sometimes qualities of voice are indicated by comparison with the voices of animals. In *Persians* 13 and *Agamemnon* 449 the verb *baúzein* implies that the speakers used a tone like that of a dog baying. Electra describes Clytemnestra as 'yelping' (*hulakteî*) in Sophocles' *Electra* 299, and in *Alcestis* 760 Heracles' drunken songs are deprecated with the same verb, there perhaps implying 'yowl'. But perhaps these pejorative terms are indications of a hostile attitude on the part of those that use them rather than of a precisely identified tone of voice.

Finally, even though our knowledge of ancient 'delivery' is so scanty, and though so much of what has been said in this chapter is speculative, we should not ignore its potentialities for *páthos*. The six elements constituted a kind of sub-musical accompaniment to the conceptual meaning of the words, except that in their case the sub-music was an integral part of the meaning, and the words could not exist without it. Modern producers of poetic drama often rely more on 'noises-off' than on this subtle word-music. In a film of *Romeo and Juliet* when Romeo said

> It was the lark, the herald of the morn,
> No nightingale. . . .,

the director helpfully added the sound of a lark singing in the background. The Greek poets could make their words sing, or weep, by themselves.

CHAPTER SIX

The visual element

The Greek words for theatre and audience (*théatron* and *theataí*, first found in fifth-century authors) imply that people went to the performances to see rather than to hear. That presumably was what happened in the early period of the Bacchic cult when the ritual ceremonies and dances mattered most. But when master-poets took over from priests and dancers, this was bound to change. Poets are artists in words not in visual effects. Before the drama developed in the sixth century BC the dominant literary entertainers in Greece were the epic rhapsodists and the lyric singers who had no need of anything except voice, music and body-movements, to present their poetry – no scenery, no stage properties. They could rely on the lively imaginations of their audiences to visualize whatever scenes the poetry described. In the fifth century the poets, who controlled the production of their own plays would naturally concentrate their chief efforts on what they could best use – the spoken word and song.

Aristotle confirms this low valuation of the visual element (*ópsis*) in the classical theatre. In his *Poetics* he says little or nothing about scenery, costume, masks, gestures, poses, groupings and choreography. He reiterates his assertion that the power and pleasure of a tragedy can be enjoyed by simply reading it (aloud) for oneself (*Poetics* 1450b, 18–20; 1453b, 4; 1462a, 12) – a most comforting assertion for us who cannot witness or reconstruct the ancient productions. Aristotle does indeed grant that certain kinds of *ópsis* could have an emotional effect, as will be discussed later, and he does not go so far as the scholiast on Sophocles' *Electra* 1404 who observes that the death-cry avoids the 'vulgarity' (*tò phortikón*) of *ópsis*. But he

confines almost all his attention to the aspects of tragedy that
need no scenic support. All the major ancient writers on drama
tacitly adopt his attitude, preferring to write about diction,
rhythm, music, plot and *psuchagōgía*. Consequently we have
to rely mainly on late lexicographers, commentators and
biographers, for information about the visual elements, or else
deduce them from the words of the dramas themselves.

The Greek psychologists, too, held that hearing was a more
emotive sense than seeing, as has already been noticed. (On the
other hand it was recognized that seeing was more convincing
to the intellect – 'Seeing is believing' – as is emphasized in
Herodotos, 1, 8, and Horace, *Art of Poetry* 180–2. But the
Greek drama was not a drama of illusion.) There are good
physiological reasons why sounds should affect our emotions
more deeply than sights. Infants can hear before they can see.
They may even have sensations akin to hearing in the pre-natal
state when they live among life-rhythms in the dark warmth of
the womb. They express their earliest feelings by cries, not by
bodily movements. In our adult years sight fails us in the dark
or when we sleep, but hearing does not. We can close our eyes
at some horrible or disgusting event, but not our ears. We can
see only what is in front of us or at our side (unlike some
animals), but we can hear from all round us. We can hear things
more clearly from a distance than we can see them – a most
important consideration in the enormous Greek theatres.
Inside us the workings of our inner organs make themselves
known to us by audial and tactile sensations and not by sight.
The vibrations of sound merge into our sense of touch, and the
rhythms of our heart and bloodstream can resemble those of
music and poetry. Most important of all for our thesis here,
animals and human beings express their strongest feelings more
subtly by cries and songs than by bodily movements, and they
give the alarm most effectively by audial means.

It is necessary to emphasize these basic principles because we
now live in a world in which visual elements have much more
influence and control than in ancient Greece – a world of traffic
lights and cameras and advertising displays. And we are

accustomed to theatres with elaborate sets, props and lighting-effects. In our theatres and television stations huge teams are concerned with making the performances *look* right, and often their interest in poetry is small, as many recent productions of Shakespeare and of the Greek dramatists have shown. Poet-dramatists had nothing like that to contend with in ancient Athens. Besides, from the time of Pythagoras the Greeks had been greatly interested in the nature and properties of sound both as a physical phenomenon and as a literary medium. They knew much less about the mysterious nature of light, though they regarded it as the most divine of physical sensations.

All this emphasis on the supreme value of the audial elements in Greek tragedy is not intended to suggest that visual effects were negligible. Even Aristotle concedes that *ópsis* can arouse pity and fear (*Poetics* 1450b, 16–20; 1453b, 1–11). In the last of these passages he seems to describe (the text is uncertain) a special, and not highly estimable, kind of tragedy which exploited spectacular scenes, citing as examples a *Prometheus* (probably Aeschylus') and a play, or plays, showing 'the things that take place in Hades'. But he is less likely to be referring to scenery than to spectacular actions such as the impaling of Prometheus and the punishment of sinners in Hell. Similarly when the *Life of Aeschylus* states that he excelled in using *ópsis* for the sake of causing *ékplēxis*, probably the author does not mean elaborate scenes and stage-properties, but rather the monstrous creatures like the 'bronze-cast griffon-eagles' and 'tawny cock-horses' that Aristophanes mocks in *Frogs* 928–38. Only two such monsters appear in his extant plays – the cow-headed Io in *Prometheus* and the Erinyes in *Eumenides*.

The famous panic in the theatre at the hideous Erinyes as described in the *Life* has often been taken as a totally visual effect. In fact Aeschylus had begun an elaborate imaginary build-up at the end of *Libation-bearers* when Orestes screams out a description of his vision of a crowd of Gorgonlike creatures clothed in dusky garments, with snakes in their hair and blood dripping from their eyes. The chorus do not see them then, but Orestes' descriptions cause disturbance (*taragmós*) in their hearts. At the beginning of *Eumenides* the crescendo of audial and imagined horror grows when the Pythian priestess comes crawling out of the temple in a state of abject terror. She, like Orestes, compares the Erinyes to Gorgons, but adds a further comparison with the loathsome Harpies as depicted in a presumably well-known painting of the disgusting feast of Phineus. Black in colour, they snort, she says, with repulsive emissions of breath and their eyes drip with a foul ooze. After the Pythia has built up this hideous mental picture, Apollo also expresses his loathing of these 'savages', these creatures 'fit-to-be-spat-at' such as even animals would avoid (67–70). Still the Erinyes do not actually rise into full view. Aeschylus, that master of fearful or pitiful suspense, does not let them show themselves in all their ghastliness until another seventy lines have passed, during which they utter the weird sounds that we have already considered, and the Ghost of Clytemnestra describes their scorching and shrivelling breath. Plainly, then, the panic in the theatre could have been the result of much more than the visual effects.

Aeschylus, Sophocles and Euripides may have learnt a lesson from the disruption in the theatre caused by that *ópsis*. At any rate in subsequent tragedies the worst horrors are described not displayed (with the possible exception of Prometheus' impalement). As they no doubt fully recognized, *ékplēxis* can be hostile to the truer tragic emotions. Perhaps it was for this reason principally that violent deaths on scene were generally avoided. Modern writers on Greek tragedy have insisted more on other reasons – a religious tabu (but Ajax, Evadne, Heracles, Hippolytos and Alcestis die on-scene); the handicap of having one out of three actors out of action (but Aeschylus used only two in several of his final scenes); aesthetic objections (but the Athenians were used to the butchery of war and of animal sacrifice); avoidance of causing excessive feelings of *philanthrōpía* (but it is questionable whether *seeing* undeserved sufferings would do that more than hearing them vividly described). No, the primary reason

was, I believe, the wish to stir the emotions most effectively –
by words not by appearances.

A comparison with Shakespeare's dramaturgy may help
here. Besides his well-known paucity of scenery, he clearly
believed that for the purpose of arousing and maintaining
emotions in his audiences words were better than visual
actions. In *Julius Caesar*, for example, the actual killing and its
immediate consequences are presented very briefly, while
Antony's highly emotive speeches about the murder are
lengthily protracted. Certainly Shakespeare elsewhere uses
visual effects more freely than the Greeks, with his on-scene
blindings and duels and stabbings. But his paramount dramatic
instruments are rhetoric and poetry.

The many problems connected with Greek scenery, stage
properties and costume have been extensively considered
elsewhere, though not much with regard to their emotional
effects. Theoretically the artists who painted the scene-
building and the *periaktoi* could have given them a saddening,
frightening or gladdening appearance, especially when the
palace of the participants was prominent in the drama as in the
Oresteia. But there is no evidence that the ancient Greeks did
that. Besides, the more distant members of an Athenian
audience would be unable to distinguish anything subtle of that
kind. Once again it was the words that had to create atmosphere and indicate locality, as in Prometheus' invocation to
nature.

So, too, with scenes of physical catastrophe, like the earth-
quakes to be noticed later in this chapter. In our cinemas and
theatres we are used to elaborate and costly representations of
vast buildings falling in shatters to the ground, terrible
tempests, appalling floods. In the Theatre of Dionysos, such
catastrophes existed only in the descriptions and movements of
the actors and choruses (which were probably more expressive
than mimetic). This is psychologically true to life. To quote a
personal experience: when the present writer experienced an
earthquake in Greece the most alarming thing was not the
actual shake but the fear expressed in the flight of all the Greeks

to get outside the building as fast as possible while we were still in a state of *ékplēxis*.

Costume was likely enough to have been used to augment emotionalism in the ancient Greek theatre – comic costume to make people laugh (as at the beginning of *Frogs*), tragic to make them cry, sinister to make them fear, hideous to cause disgust and *tarachē* (as in the combination of loathsomeness and terror in the appearance of the Erinyes). Notoriously Euripides exploited the pathos of presenting heroes and heroines in rags – Telephos, Oineus, Bellerophon and Philoctetes in lost plays, and Electra, Hecuba and Menelaos in those that survive. (Aeschylus, who mocks Euripides for this in *Frogs* 1063–5, avoided the visual representation of such indignities in *Persians* 849–51 by making the Queen bring a change of clothes to the ragged Xerxes before he appeared on scene.) But Sophocles was not above using similar emblems of misery in *Philoctetes* 274 and *Oedipus at Colonos* 1258. Colour symbolism could be effective here – the regular dark clothes for mourners (Jocasta's dress is both black and torn in *Phoenician Women* 324–6), the dusky clothes of the Erinyes in the *Oresteia*, the black clothes of Death in *Alcestis*, and possibly the saffron-coloured dress of Iphigeneia in *Agamemnon* 239. If Agamemnon's robes were blood-coloured, like the fabrics spread for him to trample, the portent would be stronger. But what was the colour of Cassandra's dress before she ripped it asunder in grief and despair?

Stage-properties could also contribute to emotionalism – old men's pitiful staves, the joyous light of torches, the awe of statues of the gods, the sorrowful associations of tombs. Often these were merely accessories to the main action, bringing quiet overtones of emotion. But other props are focal points for a whole scene – the funeral urn given to Electra, the fatal sword of Ajax, the poisoned robe in *Women of Trachis*, the bow of Philoctetes, the red fabrics strewn for Agamemnon's path to death and, most sensational of all, the heads of Pentheus in *Bacchai* and of Aigisthos in Euripides' *Electra*.

But what about the ubiquitous masks? What were their

advantages and disadvantages in emotional scenes? To modern theatre-goers the absence of facial movement might seem a severe handicap for emotional acting – and still more to cinema-goers used to gazing on pictures of faces enlarged so hugely that the slightest flutter of an eyelid or wrinkling of the forehead, or trembling of the lips or change of colour is clear to see. But was the total obliteration of the performers' faces such a loss dramatically as we might think? Unfortunately we have no evidence from the classical period to help us in answering that question. But perhaps we can learn from the opinion of a modern poet-dramatist who used masks in some of his plays. W. B. Yeats wrote in his *Essays and Introductions* (p. 226):

> A mask will enable me to substitute for the face of some commonplace player, or for that face repainted to suit his own vulgar fancy, the fine invention of a sculptor, and to bring the audience close enough to the play to hear every inflection of the voice. A mask never seems but a dirty face, and no matter how close you go is yet a work of art; nor shall we lose by stilling the movement of the features, for deep feeling is expressed by a movement of the whole body. In poetical painting and sculpture the face seems nobler for lacking curiosity, alert attention, all that we sum up under the famous word of the realists, vitality.

Some of the implications of this pronouncement are idiosyncratic. But with acute insight, derived partly from his knowledge of the Japanese Noh drama, Yeats picked out the essential feature of masked acting, its emphasis on the voice and on bodily movement rather than on facial expression. As a poet he valued the absence of distraction from the words. As a dramatist he preferred that the whole body should express emotion and not just the movements of the face.

The Greeks of the classical period would have had good reason to agree. Nuances of facial expression played little part in either their visual arts or their literature. In their sculpture and painting the whole body speaks by gesture or pose, not just the face which is often expressionless even in moments of intense grief or pain. (An exception in a painting by Timanthes will be noticed later.) In literature facial descriptions are minimal. When occasionally the face of a character is described in tragedy only one or two significant features are mentioned, like the long hair and white complexion of Dionysos in *Bacchai* 455–9, the blue-black eyebrows of Death in *Alcestis* 261, and the flashing eyes of Lyssa in *Heracles* 884. References to frowns or quivering nostrils or trembling lips are rare in Greek literature down to Hellenistic times. The same tendency to ignore facial appearance and expression holds in the New Testament. Nothing is said there about the faces of Christ and the Apostles, except by the imaginative author of the Apocalypse.

Though masks prevented the audience from seeing any changes of expression on the actors' faces, they did not entirely prevent the use of facial expression for emotive purposes. When a dramatist wanted the audience to react to such indications he told them what they were to see in their minds' eyes – tears, foaming at the mouth, hair on end, torn cheeks, paleness, redness and so on. Masks could be changed or altered after climactic events such as the blinding of Oedipus.

Yeats in the passage just quoted mentions another effect of acting in masks which could help dramatists to maintain the kind of emotionalism that they desired. Masks covered 'the face of some commonplace actor' (commonplace, presumably, in comparison with the uncommonplace poet-playwright). The cult of the actor in the modern theatre has often worked against the author's intentions. People go to see So-and-so playing Hamlet rather than Shakespeare's *Hamlet*. Worse still, the whole production of a play may be adapted to suit the star actor's style and mannerisms. In the later period of Greek tragedy a similar ascendancy of the actors apparently developed. (Voices could be identified behind the masks, and gestures could have a personal style.) Indeed actors' interpolations – inserted no doubt to 'improve' theatricality – played havoc with some dramatic texts. (It is said that 'the Shakespeare of the Japanese theatre', Takeda Izumo, preferred to have his plays performed by puppets, with the words spoken off-scene, in order to eliminate intrusive histrionics.)

Pictorial evidence has survived from antiquity to show that actors solemnly contemplated the masks of the characters they were playing. If so, the mask could deepen their emotional involvement with their roles. Perhaps, too, the classical actors went through a ceremony of prayers and libations to the god of the theatre before assuming their masks, as Mary Renault so vividly imagines in *The Mask of Apollo*. Such a solemn process would have a psychological effect on an actor that would be quite different from what happens when he looks into a mirror and repaints his face, in Yeats's words, 'to suit his own vulgar fancy'. A mask designed by an artist on the advice of the dramatist would impose its dramatic implications on the actor, while 'make-up' allows him to follow his own fancies and perhaps his own egotism. In an ideal production make-up will be in full harmony with the mood of the play. But too often it makes the actor look like what he, or she, wants to look like, not what the author wants.

Besides giving emphasis to voices and bodily movements, masks can produce another noteworthy emotional effect. As one can still experience from witnessing oriental plays and African dances, the fixity of expression and the stylized features of masks have a strangely compelling, and almost a mesmeric, power, and at times the voice issuing from the immobile mouth seems demonic. One can perhaps best feel the horror of the masks of the Erinyes by contemplating a demon-mask from Africa. Unfortunately the surviving specimens and pictures of ancient Greek masks may not faithfully represent those of the fifth century.

Bodily movements and gestures are the most natural means of expressing emotion. We must distinguish here between those which can be acted, such as shuddering with fear or trembling with joy, and those which cannot be deliberately produced, such as paleness or hair standing on end. Accomplished actors and orators can simulate the first kind whether they feel the appropriate emotions or not. The second kind can only be described or alleged – 'I grow pale, I shiver with dread, my hair stands on end', or 'You grow pale etc.', or 'He grows pale etc.' It may be that the actor or orator is carried away by genuine emotion so that their physical reactions are truly his. But normally he can only simulate them and hope that his audience will believe him.

The Greek and Roman rhetoricians had much to say about the best gestures for indicating and arousing emotion as well as those for emphasizing thought. Quintilian in his elaborate discussion (11, 3, 65–136) describes how the head, face, arms, body and feet can express a speaker's feelings – joy, sorrow, humility, abhorrence, wonder, shame, hesitation and much else. On the other hand, he warns orators against mimetic gestures: an orator should be as unlike a dancer as possible, and his gestures should be adapted to the feelings (*sensus*) rather than to the words, 'as was the practice of the more dignified actors in the past' (11, 3, 89). Actors, he adds, should not imitate the voices of characters that they are describing, for 'some kinds of imitations are a fault even for people whose art consists entirely of imitation.'

One cannot always separate gestures of thought from gestures of feeling or from spontaneous and instinctive reactions. The two sources of expressive bodily movement, the mind and the autonomous nervous system often work together, as when we dance for joy, or clench our fists in anger, or extend our open hand in friendly welcome. Convention also rules in these actions. But it varies from tradition to tradition. We in Western Europe shake our heads from side to side in denial, while the Greeks, from as far back as Homer's time, move their heads upwards. But both we and they nod downwards in assent.

The regular gestures of strong grief in Greek tragedy are: veiling the head, beating the head and body with one's hands, tearing or cutting the hair, slashing the face and body with one's finger nails and ripping one's clothes (e.g. *Libation-bearers* 24–31, Euripides' *Suppliant Women* 110–11, and *Electra* 146–50). The gesture of veiling the face prompted a noteworthy observation by Quintilian (2, 13, 12–13) on the topic that some themes involve feelings too deep to be expressed as they deserve. He cites the famous painting of the sacrifice of Iphigeneia by Timanthes, a contemporary of Euripides. (In the Pompeian copy the facial expressions hardly tally with Quintilian's description.) The artist, he says, having portrayed three of the Greeks, Calchas, Odysseus and Menelaos, as showing an ascending scale of grief in their faces, found it impossible to render Agamemnon's supreme agony of sorrow. So he depicted him with his face veiled. Euripides uses a different method of showing extreme grief when Peleus (in *Andromache* 1076–80) and Hecuba (in *Hecuba* 486–7) fall to the ground in abject sorrow. (Homer goes further: Priam and Odysseus roll about in their grief in *Iliad* 24, 165, and *Odyssey* 10, 499).

These movements can serve as appeals for pity as well as expressions of emotion. Others are more deliberate and purposeful. When women and children are in distress they kneel and touch the cheek or beard, or tug at the robes of the person they are supplicating. Appealing for pity *in extremis* women bare their breasts – Clytemnestra both in *Libation-bearers* 896–8, and in Euripides' *Electra* 1207, as well as Polyxena in *Hecuba* 560, and Jocasta in *Phoenician Women* 1568. For Hermione in *Andromache* 822–3 it is a gesture of grief. For Helen it was a means of reviving Menelaos' passion for her beauty on their first meeting after the fall of Troy, as described in *Andromache* 629 (cf. Aristophanes, *Lysistrata* 155–6), like Phryne rather than Hecuba. In one case, but only described not enacted, a victim strips herself naked – Iphigeneia in *Agamemnon*, as will be considered in chapter 9. (It has been argued that two conditions of Greek drama prevented exposure of the breasts on the scene – the actors were male and most of the audience would be too far away to see it. But the language of the passages cited seems to require at least a gesture of disrobing.)

As signs of fear actors and choruses probably made movements of retreat and of attempted escape. We have already noticed the grotesque action of the Delphic priestess in *Eumenides* 35–8, when, appalled by the sight and sound of the Erinyes, she scrambles out of the temple on her hands and knees. It is duplicated in *Hecuba* 1058–9, where Polymestor, after he has been blinded and his two sons killed, crawls on to the scene 'like a four-footed beast of the mountain'.

In the vivid description of mixed grief and terror in *Libation-bearers* 32, we find a reference to a kind of reaction that could not be portrayed on the scene – the hair-standing on end, so, too, in *Seven* 564 and *Oedipus at Colonos* 322. This, like weeping and changes of facial expression, could only be projected into the audiences' minds, not exhibited visually. But, as already noticed, Greek audiences were well used to exercising their imaginations in that way.

Joy is normally expressed visually by high-stepping dancing or leaping. The chorus in Euripides' *Electra* 859–61 proclaim that they will raise their joyous leapings to the sky 'like deer'. When the chorus in *Ajax* (693ff.) are persuaded that their lord and master no longer intends to kill himself they say that they 'soar aloft in extreme joy' and appeal to Pan to launch them into exotic dances. So, too, the chorus in *Heracles* (762ff.) proclaim 'dances, dances and revelling' in Thebes when the wicked Lycos dies, and the Watchman in *Agamemnon* (31) announces that he himself will dance a prelude to 'the establishment of many dances in Argos' now that the news of Troy's capture has come. (As a grim contrast one may compare how Hitler used to shuffle a dance-step at news of another success.)

Affection and friendliness evoke the conventional gestures of embracing, caressing and hand-clapping. Kissing would be an awkward manoeuvre for masked actors, but it is sometimes described (*Alcestis* 402, *Trojan Women* 763, *Phoenician Women* 1671, *Heracles* 486). Disgust like Cassandra's in *Agamemnon* 1307 was visually expressed by shrinking back and perhaps by repellent movements of the hands – or more deliberately by spitting as in *Antigone* 1232. One would expect anger and hatred to be shown by characters like Oedipus, Electra, Deianeira and Medea, with aggressive movements of their arms and stiffening of their bodies, but these are not mentioned in the texts – nor are the bowed head of shame, the pointing finger of scorn and the raised arms of surprise.

All this is for actors, choruses and audiences. But authors, too, were advised by Aristotle in *Poetics* 1455a 29–30 to adopt the poses and movements of the characters and actions they were describing (as, it is said, Sir Joshua Reynolds did when painting). In other words dramatists should have a kinaesthetic sense of their subjects. Pressed to extremes this would lead to absurdities – in describing the deaths of Pentheus or Astyanax for example. But we should remember that Aeschylus and Sophocles themselves performed as actors and dancers, and the early dramatists were called 'dancers' (see Athenaios 1, 22A).

Choral dancing is organized movement and gesture. Plutarch (*Moralia* 747B) divides it into three elements, movements, postures and indications, and he says (like Aristotle in *Poetics* 1447a 27–8) that these bodily movements naturally expressed those movements of the psyche which are called emotions. We need not spend any time here on indications, such as pointing (as mentioned in *Agamemnon* 1332) as they are gestures of thought rather than of feeling. Nor need we dwell on movements and postures that could have imitated physical actions that were being described, such as the bending of the tree in *Bacchai* 1064–9, or possibly even the tearing asunder of Pentheus in the same play. In fact there is no firm evidence about the degree of mimicry that the choruses employed either when the actors were speaking or when they themselves were singing. In the first example probably it was restrained so as not to distract attention from the Messenger's words. In the second perhaps the gestures were more emphatic. But too much mimicry would verge on the comic.

As to the direct expression of emotion in the tragic dancing one may reasonably conjecture, for example, from the text of Aeschylus' *Seven* and *Suppliant Women* that the choruses mimed their panic fears. The earthquake scenes in *Prometheus* 1080ff., *Heracles* 904–5 and *Bacchai* 585ff., and the burning of Troy (*Trojan Women* 1295ff.) would lend themselves to similar movements of terror. The production of *Bacchai* by Michael Cacoyannis in New York in the autumn of 1980 proved how effective this expressive dancing could be. It also offered a satisfying answer to a problem that has vexed scholars – why is there no reference by Pentheus in the following scene to the destruction of the palace? In New York the chorus's excited replies and descriptions (in very fast rhythms), and especially the gestures and movements they employed to embody their terror and awe, totally held the audience's attention. What mattered was the emotional effect, not the fact that a building was supposed to be falling down. (In fact no scenery was used.) By the time Pentheus enters, preoccupied by his own troubles, the atmosphere of fear has been calmed and a new emotion, anger, takes over.

We should not, however, expect that classical tragedy allowed the excesses of the later mime-dances which Lucian ridiculed in his essay on the dance. In one of these called 'the Fearsome Dance' the performer made fierce lunges at the audience while he emitted alarming snorts and roars like a wild animal. Yet perhaps one dance at least in extant tragedy may have been as sensational – that of the Erinyes at the opening of *Eumenides*. If, as the *Life of Aeschylus* asserts, they moved in a scattered way (*sporádēn*) and not in the customary march-formation of a normal parodos, the *ékplēxis* would be all the stronger. Similar perhaps in movement, but not terrifying, may have been the inrush of the Bacchanals at the beginning of *Bacchai*. There the intention probably was to represent the wild energy and ecstasy of the Dionysiac cult and a sense of 'swarm-feeling'.

The choric dances had a kind of geometry of their own when the disciplined troupes of twelve or fifteen took up their positions in ordered ranks and files, like ninepins, in the stasima, or as they marched about in the anapaestic passages, at best with the kinetic precision of a company of crack infantry-men today. Some people find this sort of figure-marching emotive in a curiously abstract way, like spectators at the Trooping of the Colour in London. The ancient Greeks with

their strong sense of order, symmetry and geometrical figur-
ation would at least have experienced strong aesthetic pleasure
when such movements were well done.

CHAPTER SEVEN

Emotionalism through vocabulary and stylistic figures

When an author wants to express his feelings or the feelings of a character in his work without explicitly stating them he can select emotive synonyms for what he is describing. He can speak of his 'home' rather than his 'house' (though in North America the two terms are hardly distinguishable now), of 'glory' rather than 'fame', or 'toil' rather than 'work', of 'nestlings' rather than 'chickens', of 'father and mother' rather than 'parents', of 'husband' or 'wife' rather than that chilling but conveniently epicene word 'spouse', and so on for hundreds of other alternatives. Some fields of discourse are particularly fertile for terms indicating anger or contempt. In political propaganda English-speakers have several mono-syllabic alternatives for the names of other races – Wogs, Wops, Micks, Brits, Yanks, Frogs and Huns – all more or less equivalent to the Greek *bárbaroi*. But the Greeks generally preferred polysyllabic terms of abuse.

It is often difficult to identify gradations of emotive force in the words of a foreign language, and still more so in a language like ancient Greek in which one has to rely on limited documentary sources. Some distinctions, however, may be deduced with a fair degree of probability when there is a good range of contexts. For example, *téknon* seems to have been a warmer term for child than *país*, which could also mean 'servant' or 'slave'. So when Sophocles makes Oedipus begin his opening speech in *King Oedipus* with the words *ô tékna* it indicates the King's paternal *storgé* for the citizens of Thebes (as the scholiast notices). *Chthón*, having associations with the dreaded underworld and its dark deities, was probably a more ominous word than *gê*. *Mênis* carried stronger overtones than

91

chólos. When Orestes in *Libation-bearers* (249) called his
mother, and Creon in *Antigone* 531 called Antigone, a viper
(*échidna*), the term probably expressed more spleen than the
commoner word for a snake, *óphis*. (Echidna is personified in
Women of Trachis 1099.) If one spoke of the light as *phéngos*
(as, e.g., in *Agamemnon* 504, and Euripides' *Electra* 866) it
apparently implied more glamour than *phôs*, though it in turn
was a word of wide emotional range. The normal word for
'joy', *chará* was a warm word, but the rarer *aglaïa*, personified
as one of the Graces, was more radiant. On the other hand the
Greeks had no full equivalent for 'home': *oîkos* was essentially
a dwelling-place, *dôma* a building, and both were without such
strong associations of family affection and comfort. Perhaps
their word for 'hearth', *hestía*, came nearest to our 'home'. But
hestía had stronger religious associations as a consequence of
the cult of Hestia (the Latin Vesta), one of the twelve
Olympians.

A Greek word that has no equally emotive synonym in
English is *xénos*, generally translated as 'a stranger'. It implied a
wide nexus of social and religious principles and conventions
protected by Zeus in his capacity as Xenios, and could mean
either 'guest' or 'host', like the Latin *hospes*. *Xenophilía*
implied benevolence, hospitality and protection, in marked
contrast with the English word from the same root, 'xeno-
phobia'. Reverence for 'the stranger within the gates' of the
Fourth Commandment came third in importance in the Greek
ethical code, after duty to the gods and duty to parents.
Cassandra's appeal to the chorus in *Agamemnon* 1315 turns on
this kind of *aidôs*.

Two kinds of emotive vocabulary were precluded by the
conventions of Greek tragic diction – diminutives, which
connote such subtle variations of attitude in Greek comedy,
and 'baby-talk' like 'Mamma' and 'Pappa' (though Homer had
used 'Pappa' with charming effect in Nausicaä's request to her
father in *Odyssey* 6, 57). There is one exception to the second
prohibition. A chorus of young women call out *Mâ Gâ* in a
moment of extreme terror in Aeschylus' *Suppliant Women* (890

and 900), much as an Italian might scream 'Mamma mia!' (but the Greek women are evoking the Earth Mother). Aeschylus allows the Nurse in *Libation-bearers* 756 to mention an unseemly detail of infant behaviour (more daringly than Homer in Phoenix's description of how he nursed Achilles as a baby, in *Iliad* 9, 488–91), but her language is in lofty tragic style.

Some terms of affection in Greek tragedy may seem rather cold to us, especially the use of 'head' or 'eye', as in Antigone's opening words to her sister, literally, 'O shared self-sisterly head of Ismene' – the kind of phrase that easily lent itself to parody in Housman's *Fragment of a Greek Tragedy*. This is primarily a stylistic idiom. But perhaps it also has some affinity with the convention in Japan by which one uses more elaborately formal terms of address according as one's familiarity and affection increase.

In some respects Greek tragic diction is troublesomely ambiguous. For example, it uses the word *anér* indiscriminately for 'husband' or 'man' and *guné* for 'wife' or 'woman'. (To translate the second term as 'lady' introduces a false note.) Such ambiguities present difficulties at times. When, for example, Ajax says to Tecmessa in *Ajax* 293, '*gúnai*, silence is an adornment for *gunaixi*' is he proclaiming this typical piece of male chauvinism for wives, or for women, or for both? On the other hand when the chorus in *Agamemnon* 1625 call Aigisthos *gúnai* the tone of contemptuous male chauvinism is unmistakable and adds another twist to the man/woman antithesis in the play. (As noticed in chapter 3, a more serious kind of ambiguity lies in two words commonly used in references to emotional reactions – *phrén* and *psuché*.) Several ambiguities of this kind will be noticed in chapter 9.

From Gorgias in the fifth century BC down to the last of the Greek and Roman rhetoricians – and indeed in European education until the end of the eighteenth century – teachers and students of rhetoric paid special attention to stylistic methods of arousing the emotions of audiences, especially by 'figures of speech' and 'figures of thought'. The most effective and most noticeable of all the emotive figures of speech is repetition. (It can, of course, also serve to give intellectual emphasis in un-emotional contexts.) The Greek rhetoricians recognized its paramount importance by distinguishing no less than eight different varieties according to the frequency and position of the repeated words or phrases. By a happy chance their examples of these figures have preserved some of the most poignant fragments of Greek poetry, as when Demetrios *On Style* (140–1) cites as an example of anadiplosis Sappho's

> Maidenhood, maidenhood, where have you gone
> and left me?
> Never again shall I come to you, never again shall I come,

and as an example of anaphora,

> Evening star, bringing home all that gleaming
> dawn has scattered:
> You bring the sheep, you bring the goat, you
> bring the child back to his mother.

Repetitions of single words and phrases occur in most of the more emotional scenes of Greek tragedy. The maximum number of single-word repetitions is in the first articulate utterance of the Erinyes, in *Eumenides* 130, 'Take, take, take, take' (perhaps derived from huntsmen's cries when urging hounds on to the kill). It equals Lear's angry 'Howl, howl, howl, howl', but falls short of his pitiful 'Never, never, never, never, never'. Sophocles comes next with the weary 'Toil, toil, toil' (with *polúptoton*) and 'Where, where, where?' of the chorus in *Ajax* 866–8. Single repetitions are commonest in the later plays of Euripides (who is ridiculed for them in *Frogs* 1352ff.), but Aeschylus and Sophocles also use them. Sometimes the repeated words are spaced out, like the slow tolling of a bell. There is an impressive example of this in *Persians* 550–2 where that name once so full of dread to Athenian ears, Xerxes, is placed at the beginning of three successive lines:

> Xerxes led them, *popoi*,
> Xerxes destroyed them, *totoi*,

Xerxes by his ill plans
Brought doom on the seafaring barks.

Such repetitions gain strength when the repeated clauses are in
rhyme and are isometric, as there and often elsewhere.

Repetitions are particularly frequent in scenes of lamentation. In *Persians* 1000ff. almost every second line is repetitious.
The effect is like that of a ritual of mourning, as mentioned in
chapter 4. One may compare the repetitions in David's lament
at the death of his darling, but rebellious, son, Absalom, in 2
Samuel 19, 4 which ends

O my son, Absalom, my son, my son Absalom!
Would I had died for you, O Absalom, my son,
my son!

Repetitions can carry other emotions besides grief. Ecstatic
joy is the mood in *Ajax* 694–5 with its lively fourfold invocation of Pan. In the repetitions of Aeschylus' *Suppliant Women*
the dominant emotion is fear. When Pentheus in *Bacchai* 655
tells Dionysos 'You're clever, clever, except where you should
be clever', the tone is angry and sarcastic like that of
an impatient schoolmaster with an exasperating pupil. On
the other hand when in the same play (116) the chorus cry
'To the mountain, to the mountain' their feeling is one of
póthos.

The most emphatic of all forms of repetition is the refrain, in
which one or more lines are repeated once, or more often, in
close proximity. Here again Aeschylus shows outstanding
skill, and is duly mocked for it by Euripides in *Frogs* 1264ff,
though in fact he occasionally used them himself (but not
Sophocles). In the opening chorus of *Suppliant Women* the
panic-stricken Danaids use three consecutive refrains, two of
four short lines and one of three, to express their fears. There
are four refrains in the *Oresteia*, varying in length from one line
to eight. The first, repeated twice and containing in itself a
repetition comes in the chorus's apprehensive song in
Agamemnon 121, 139 and 159:

> Say 'Woe for Linos, Woe for Linos,' but let the
> good prevail.

The name of Linos – perhaps that of a beautiful youth who died
tragically – seems to have carried strong associations of grief
and may have been a traditional element in ancient Greek ritual
mourning. It recurs in sorrowful contexts in *Ajax* 628 and
Orestes 1395. An equivalent in English literature is the Willow
Song so poignantly employed by Shakespeare to convey the
grief of Ophelia and Desdemona.

The second refrain in *Agamemnon* (1489–96, 1513–20) is the
longest and the most moving in all Greek tragedy: Its three
inner repetitions raise the emotional power to a uniquely high
degree:

> Oh, Oh, King, King,
> How shall I weep for you?
> What can I say from my loving heart?
> There you lie in the web of the spider –
> Woe for me, for me – on that ignoble bed,
> Slain in a treacherous doom
> From a hand with a two-edged blade.

Whatever the audience may have thought of Agamemnon in
the earlier part of the play, when they heard this dirge sung
twice – with the tones and gestures of ritual lamentation and to
the mournful music of the pipe and in full view of the corpses of
the murdered victims – who could have failed to feel a deep
surge of tragic grief?

In complete contrast, the refrain in *Libation-bearers* 961–4
and 971a–d (if the manuscripts are to be interpreted in this way)
proclaims the joy of the chorus at Orestes' revenge on
Clytemnestra and Aigisthos:

> Look, the light is breaking!
> The chain that curbed the halls gives way
> Rise up, proud house, long, too long
> your walls lay fallen, strewn along the earth
> (Robert Fagles's translation)

Quite different again is the emotional effect of the six-line refrain in *Eumenides* 328–33 and 341–6. Being part of the 'binding song' of the Erinyes, it is permeated with the magical and incantatory power of witches' spells and ritual cursings:

> Over the victim's burning head
> this chant, this strain, driving frenzy
> striking madness crazing the mind,
> this hymn of Fury,
> chaining the senses, ripping across the lyre,
> withering lives of men
>
> (Robert Fagles's translation)

It is significant that refrains also play a prominent part in the best account of black magic in extant Greek poetry, Theocritos' second *Idyll*.

When words are repeated after a long interval, as will be exemplified in chapter 9, the effect is naturally weakened, and it is often hard to judge whether the repetition was meant to be noticeable or not. The epithet 'new-slaughtered' is used twice in *Ajax* (546 and 898), first with reference to the cattle killed by Ajax and second to Ajax himself after his corpse has been discovered. Were the audience expected to feel that Ajax has been paid in kind for killing the cattle – 'the biter bitten'? Generally scholars have been inclined to treat such repetitions as fortuitous. But we should not underestimate the alertness of Athenian audiences or the stylistic subtlety of the master-dramatists. Much would depend on the degree of emphasis given to the repeated words by the actor and on the rarity of the words. If Shakespeare had repeated 'incarnadine' in *Macbeth* after its use by Macbeth in Act Two it would hardly have been accidental. Possibilities of that kind will be considered further in chapter 9.

Next in emotional power to repetition is apostrophe, a 'turning away' from the main tenor of discourse to address some person or thing not directly involved in the action, as in Antony's

> O Judgment! Thou art fled to brutish beasts. . . .,

and Cicero's famous *O tempora, O mores*! These express indignation and regret. In Euripides, *Electra* 866–7, it expresses Electra's unholy joy at the death of Aigisthos – 'O radiant light, O flashing chariot of the sun, O earth and night . . .', and Medea exults after she has persuaded Aigeus to help her in similar terms, 'O Zeus, and Justice of Zeus, and light of the sun' (*Medea* 764). Apostrophe is specially apt when a character feels alone in grief, as in Philoctetes' appeal to his cave (1081–90), Antigone's outburst to her tomb (891–2), Oedipus' cry to the darkness that now covers his eyes (1313) and Ajax's bitter invocation (394–400) of the light that is now, metaphorically, darkness for him. (Lonely grief is also finely expressed in the cry of Prometheus to 'the divinely bright sky, the swift-winged breezes, the fountains of the rivers, the uncountable laughter of the ocean's waves, and the all-seeing circle of the sun' (88–91). But this is an invocation rather than an apostrophe, since Prometheus has not spoken before in the play – the two figures, however, are not always clearly distinguishable.)

The rhetoricians also thought well of aposiopesis, that is, falling silent without finishing one's sentence, as a means of expressing emotion. Quintilian (9, 2, 54) asserts that an orator can use it for passion, anger or anxiety. In drama it has a wider scope. When Philoctetes is attacked by spasms of pain (731) he first falls silent and then he breaks his sentences with the screams noticed in chapter 4 (732–54 and cf. 785–84). The Messenger in *King Oedipus* 1289 begins to describe the King as 'his mother's . . .', but cannot bring himself to say 'husband'. The chorus in *Agamemnon* 498 shrink from mentioning the possibility that the beacons signal a defeat at Troy, for fear of ill omen. Cassandra's particularly pathetic aposiopesis in *Agamemnon* 1315 will be considered in chapter 9.

Strong feelings can be indicated by other disturbances of normal syntax (cf. Demetrios, *On Style* 194), such as failure to continue a construction (*anakólouthon*) as in *Seven against*

Thebes 435, 'Send against such a man . . . who will withstand him?') or absence of conjunctions (*asúndeton*) as in *Antigone* 876–7, 'Unwept, unbefriended, unwedded, wretched in heart', and dislocation of normal word-order (*huperbatón*). This last is harder to identify in ancient Greek since its word-order is much freer than in English and other European languages. But it is unmistakably operative in such extreme cases as in *Heracles* 431–4: 'The with-no-return-to-home, of the children, of-Charon-awaits-the-boat, of-life-the-path . . .' (that is, 'The boat of Charon awaits the children's path of life that offers no return'). Also, without being grammatically irregular, jerky syntax often indicates emotion, as Aeschylus both exemplifies and affirms in *Seven against Thebes* 806 when the Chorus ask

Who? What did you say? I am distraught in speech by fear.

Emotional excitement can also be indicated by the division of lines between two speakers (*antilabé*). The most extreme type is exemplified in *Bacchai* 1181 where the chorus and the frenzied Agave cry out like this

> *Chorus.* What other?
> *Agave.* Of Cadmos . . .
> *Chorus.* Of Cadmos?
> *Agave.* His children.

(referring to the slayers of Pentheus) with a similar (but bitterly ironic) interchange in 1197. (Each of the eight words forms a baccheios, most aptly for this intensely Bacchic scene.) There are equally fast interchanges when the chorus in *Oedipus at Colonos* 524ff. with horrified curiosity question Oedipus about his abominable acts. Sophocles occasionally, but rarely, breaks his trimeters into three or four at moments of high emotional tensity in stichomythia (*Philoctetes* 753, 810, 814, 816, *King Oedipus* 684, *Oedipus at Colonos* 539, 546, 832). Division between two speakers is common in both Sophocles and Euripides, but not in Aeschylus (except in *Prometheus* 980, if that play is by Aeschylus). Stichomythia itself, even without being broken by *antilabḗ*, regularly denotes increased excitement.

Three kinds of questions can be used emotionally. 'Aporetic' questions – like 'What shall I do, where shall I go?, etc. – are often used to indicate a pathetic state of helplessness. Failure to answer a direct question is a sign of anxious self-absorption on the part of Agamemnon in *Iphigeneia at Aulis* 2–19 and of others elsewhere. But the most celebrated example of failure to heed what is being said is in *King Oedipus* 717ff. where Oedipus fails to react to Jocasta's remark about the pierced feet of Laios' son because her previous reference to the fatal crossroads has caused 'wandering and upheaval in his *psuchḗ*'. Rhetorical questions are often designed more for intellectual emphasis than for emotionalism. But they, too, can carry pathos, as when Megara in *Heracles* 280–1 exclaims

> I love my children, for how could I not love
> Those I have borne and travailed for?

In contrast with the kind of emotional response that consists in saying too little, the reverse, saying too much, can also indicate tense feelings. 'Pleonasm' and 'tautology' are the main rhetorical terms for this. Aeschylus is pilloried in *Frogs* 1152–76 for using phrases like 'hear and listen', 'I arrive and return' – unfairly again because such doublets can increase a sense of solemnity and urgency especially in solemn supplications. They were a regular feature of Hebrew poetry, as in the Psalmist's 'Give ear and hearken unto my prayer.' The other tragedians also use tautologies and pleonasms fairly often, but more for emphasis (and metre, perhaps) than for solemnity.

Aristotle states in *Rhetoric* 1408b 19 that compound words and accumulations of epithets accord with the emotional style and may be used by orators when they have roused their audiences to a state of *enthousiasmós*. Aeschylus certainly seems to have agreed, to judge by the strings of compound epithets that he unleashes from time to time – 'a groan, heart-rending, self-mourning, self-grieving, mind-destroying, unjoyous, tear-pouring' in *Seven against Thebes* 916–920, 'breezes . . . bringing-harmful-leisure, hungry, anchorage-spoiling . . . unsparing of ships and cables, making the time double-length' (*Agamemnon* 192–6). At the climax of the Prophet's first announcements in *Agamemnon* 146–55 there are three groups of accumulated epithets, 'preventions-of-sailings due-to-adverse-winds, lengthy, ship-holding . . .', 'another-kind-of feast, unsanctioned-by-custom, offering no banquet, inborn constructor of quarrels, not man- (or husband)-fearing' . . ., and 'wrath, fearful, resurgent, house-keeping, crafty, remembering, child-avenging' – a tremendous crescendo towards the dominant theme of hereditary evil. Though Sophocles and Euripides sometimes accumulate compound epithets in that way they never dare anything so tremendous.

If we ask what kind of effect Aeschylean turgidity might have had on Athenians in the first half of the fifth century we must remember that the dithyrambic and Dionysiac tradition was still strong at that time. Also we should recall that, according to Aristotle, such language was emotionally effective when an audience was in a state of *enthousiasmós*, unlike the condition of Quintilian. For us in our time, when authors tend so much to avoid extravagant language it is hard to appreciate the effect of exotic language of this climactic kind – and it is all too easily parodied. It certainly violates the rule of 'Nothing in excess'. But, as already emphasized, tragedy flourishes on excess.

In fact the name of a favourite figure of the tragedians, hyperbole, means excess. (In it we move from 'figures of language' to the so-called 'figures of thought'.) The rhetoricians considered it specially apt for expressing anger: Oedipus uses it angrily to Teiresias in *King Oedipus* 371

> You're blind in your ears, blind in your mind,
>   blind in your eyes,

and Antigone in *Oedipus at Colonos* 1745,

> Desperate then, and even more than desperate.

Hyperbolical language is not in favour among serious present-day authors. Nor, except in the works of James Joyce and his followers, is paronomasia – a figure whose title has been trivialized into 'punning' and 'playing on words'. Paronomasia could be profoundly serious and pathetic in antiquity, and indeed until the time of Shakespeare. Examples of tragic paronomasia have been extensively studied elsewhere. It is most commonly used with proper names. 'Helen' is interpreted as 'Hell to ships, hell to men, hell to cities' (with asyndeton) in *Agamemnon* 689–90. Pentheus is seen as containing *pénthos*, 'grief', in *Bacchai* 508, and later (1244) Cadmos will cry out 'Oh immeasurable *pénthos*'. Ajax begins his first coherent speech in *Ajax* 430–1 with the rhetorical question '*Aiai* . . . who would have thought that my name [Aias in the Greek] would be so apt for my woes?'

The emotional impact of paronomasia is less powerful, but not negligible, when it is not based on a proper name, and no personal destiny is involved. In the stanza after the interpretation of 'Helen', the chorus observes that 'only too truly' she brought *kêdos* to Troy, for the word can mean both 'grief' and 'a marriage bond'. (King Charles I of England expressed his concern in a similar figure when the Duke of Hamilton addressed him in his troubles as 'My dear master'. He replied 'I have been a *dear* master to you indeed.') The fact that *chaîre* meant both 'farewell' and 'rejoice' permitted a poignant equivocation in several parting scenes in tragedy. In *Bacchai* 1379–80 Agave bids her father '*Chaîre*' in the sense of farewell. He bids her '*Chaîre*' in return and then, taking the word in its other sense, he adds, 'But it would be hard for you to attain to that' (cf. *Hecuba* 426–7, *Electra* 1357–9).

Plutarch in discussing special meanings and functions of words in his essay on how to study poetry (*Moralia* 25A) says that 'much disturbance and confusion (*taraché*) is caused by such phrases in Euripides as 'a painful happy life' (*Medea* 598) and 'that happy iniquity, tyranny' (*Phoenician Women* 549). He means mental confusion principally, but such oxymora, with their element of paradox, can also convey emotional disturbance, as when the chorus in *Prometheus* 904–5 describes *érōs* as 'causing a no-war war' and bringing a 'no-means means' (*apólemos pólemos, ápora pórimos*). Similarly Ajax bitterly remarks (665) about the sword given to him by Hector (which will soon be the means of his suicide), 'The gifts of enemies are no-gifts' (*ádora dôra*). Orestes epitomizes a whole chapter of grief and destruction when he describes Troy as a 'non-city city' (*ápolin pólin, Eumenides* 457). Sometimes these oxymora almost amount to enigmas, for example in Aeschylus' recurrent phrase *cháris ácharis* (*Prometheus* 545, *Agamemnon* 1545, cf. *Libation-bearers* 42). It is all the harder to translate because *cháris* itself is a highly complex term (and sometimes has sexual implications). Oxymora of this kind generally indicate a state of heart and mind in which words have lost their normal meanings and the established state of things has gone awry. A specially poignant example comes in the bizarre passage in *Alcestis* 348–54 where Admetos tells his wife that as soon as she dies for him he will have an image of her made to place in his bed and to adore and embrace –

A chilly joy (*térpsis*) but yet I think it may avail
For me to drain away my heart's (*psuchês*) sad weight.

A similar figure is paradox. But it serves to stimulate intellectual interest rather than emotional feeling, as when the Maidservant in *Alcestis* 141 provokes the curiosity of the chorus by saying that the Queen is 'both living and dead', and when both Aeschylus and Sophocles make characters say 'the dead is slaying the living' (*Libation-bearers* 886, *Women of Trachis* 1111, 1163) the explanation being – as all alert Athenians would understand – that Orestes was deemed to be dead before he killed his mother, and it was the poison of the dead Centaur Nessos that killed Heracles.

An aspect of Greek tragic diction that was not identified by the ancient rhetoricians and literary critics has received special attention in recent times – the use of abstract terms, especially those ending in -*ma*, to express emotional attitudes towards persons. Sophocles uses it with special success. So Electra calls

Clytemnestra 'a thing of hate (*mísēma*) and the Queen in turn calls her 'a shameless product of nurture' (*thrémm' anaidés*) in *Electra* 289 and 622; Creon insults Haimon as 'a women's slave-piece' (*doúleuma*) in *Antigone* 756; and Ajax vilifies Odysseus as 'the instrument (*órganon*) of all evils' (*Ajax* 380). Such terms are often hard to translate satisfactorily in English. Perhaps the tone of the childish phrase 'You nasty thing' comes closest to their effect when used in contempt, anger and denunciation. But they are also employed at times in expressions of joy, as in *Philoctetes* 234 and *Oedipus at Colonos* 324–5.

One further figure deserves attention. As Demetrios observed in his treatise on style (99–100), ambiguities and double meanings can be menacing and alarming. He calls this *allēgoría*, 'saying something else as well'. He quotes as an example the remark of Dionysios of Syracuse to the Locrians that 'their cicadas would sing from the ground', meaning that he would cut down all their trees and vines. Aeschylus is particularly adept in using these amphibolies to cause *tarachē* and apprehension, as will be illustrated in chapter 9. They differ from the double meanings of dramatic irony in that the speaker is fully conscious of the second meaning as well as of the first.

Other figures are mentioned by the rhetoricians as being useful for expressing and arousing emotion. But those described in this chapter are the chief devices used by the tragedians. Many of them may not have been identified and classified until the great age of Greek tragedy was over. But, like the good Monsieur Jourdain in Molière's *Bourgeois Gentilhomme* with his untutored ability to speak in prose, poets had been employing these figures freely and effectively since Homer.

It should not be overlooked that there is a fundamental difference between all such rhetorical methods of expressing and arousing emotion and the aural and visual methods described in the previous chapters (though the two methods can be combined). Figures of speech and thought appeal directly to the mind. They serve primarily to emphasize a statement or to stimulate mental effort. We must actively and intelligently co-operate with them. In contrast the aural and visual elements in drama – such as rhythm, melody, noise, colour, movement – speak directly to our senses in ways that are more primitive than language itself, ways to which birds, beasts and fishes react. So when Demetrios (*On Style* 57) says that the particle *dé* can express *páthos*, taking the place of an emotional exclamation, we must make a distinction. It is true, of course, that this particle is often used in emotional passages in tragedy, as the standard work on the Greek particles fully illustrates. But in terms of emotional impact there is obviously a vast difference between the Greek *ai ai* or the Irish *ochone, ochone*, uttered at a moment of extreme grief, and a statement like 'My son is indeed dead.' The exclamatory cries speak directly to the heart. The emphatic statement speaks to the head. But here again we are, perhaps, separating thought from feeling in the *psuché* too sharply. When an electrical storm is directly overhead the illuminating flash of the lightning and the terrifying roll of the thunder merge in one experience, though when we are at a distance they seem to be quite separate. In this book we are looking at emotional effects at a distance. At a masterly performance in the theatre there would be no questions about brain-language and heart-language.

CHAPTER EIGHT

Emotionalism through subject-matter, imagery, irony and structure

Undeniably the violent incidents described in several Greek tragedies are utterly atrocious. A frenzied mother tears her son to pieces (*Bacchai*). A jealous woman contrives the death of her innocent rival by giving her a dress anointed with a magical drug that eats away her flesh to the bone (*Medea*). Fathers are tricked into eating their own children (*Tereus, Thyestes*). Daughters persuade their father to allow himself to be boiled to death in the hope of rejuvenation (*Peliades*). King Minos is killed in a scalding bath (*Kamikoi*). Prometheus has a stake driven through his body. Oedipus marries his mother after killing his father. Children are murdered by parents, parents by children, husbands by wives, brothers by brothers – all satisfying Aristotle's principle that deeds of violence have the strongest emotional effect when they take place among next-of-kin.

These are Grand Guignol themes, hardly surpassed in atrocity by those of the most horrific films of our time. The tragedians did not hesitate to describe frightful details – the blood spurting out from the victim's veins in *Agamemnon* 1389–90 and *Ajax* 918–19, the poison eating and burning its way through the flesh in *Women of Trachis* 766–71 and *Medea* 1189–1203 where 'The flesh, consumed by the poison's hidden jaws, flowed away from the bones like resin weeping from a pinetree.' One of the most gruesome touches of all comes in *Agamemnon* 1594–6 where we are told how Atreus carefully removed the fingers and toes from the dish of children's flesh that he served to their father.

There were, of course, mitigating circumstances in the presentation of these ghastly events. First, there was the fact that they were usually not seen in the play, so that the physical *ékplēxis* of actually witnessing such horrors was avoided. Secondly, they were described in disciplined poetic diction, not in crude prose. Thirdly, they were not presented amorally, as they so often are in the modern theatre and cinema, but were generally condemned by the chorus or by characters in the play. Fourthly, the sufferings of the victims, even when they themselves were responsible, were accompanied by pity and grief from others in the play. (Out-and-out villains are not fit for tragedy, as Aristotle observed.)

Yet the Greeks must have enjoyed hearing about these atrocious happenings, or else the tragedians, eager to win the prize as well as to construct a work of art, would hardly have continued to present them so vividly. There is no evidence for any lessening of horrifics in the fifth century. Euripides exploited them as fully as Aeschylus. Why did the Athenians enjoy them? The least creditable motive could have been *epichairekakía* as described on an earlier page. There is probably some of this enjoyment of other people's sufferings in many more people than would care to admit it, as the popularity of crude violence in modern theatres and cinemas attests. However, no ancient critic suggests that this vicious pleasure contributed to the emotional effect of tragedy, though later theories about the comic catharsis regarded it as a constituent in that process. The main reason for the paradoxical enjoyment of witnessing sad events probably lay elsewhere. From the time of Homer onwards Greek poets recognized that tears and grief about past events could give pleasure. We speak of tears as 'a relief', but the Greeks regarded weeping as positively pleasurable in itself, provided that it was not accompanied by physical pain.

In the same way fear can be paradoxically enjoyable provided one is not afraid of an actual present danger. Greek tragedy seldom portrayed its scenes of pain and violence in the realistic way of the modern theatre where audiences can be really and painfully terrified. Also it almost always presented the *páthos* as a past event – except for the death-cries. This avoidance of immediacy would reduce the element of shock and pain in each *páthos*. The tragic events took place in the theatre of the mind and heart, not in the physical theatre.

A poet-dramatist has a subtler means of playing on his hearer's emotions than by narrating emotive stories. He can use metaphors, similes and comparisons, that evoke automatic and sometimes unconscious responses. Quintilian (8, 6, 19) affirms that metaphor is capable of 'thoroughly moving the spirit' (*permovendis animis*: the context shows that he meant in an emotional way) as well as giving significance and vividness. Emotionally metaphor gets its effects chiefly in two special ways, by symbolism and by personification. Metaphors and, in a weaker way, similes acquire emotional power either by evoking memories or by stimulating subliminal reactions coming from innate or inbred psychological patterns. To cite a frequent example: to compare someone to the Gorgon Medusa would automatically cause a *frisson* of fear among Athenians familiar with frightful stories and pictures of that vampire-toothed petrifying monster. Aeschylus, born and bred in an age when thought was still symbolical rather than logical, excels in that emotive kind of imagery. He is particularly fond of animal symbolisms, using them to evoke both fear and pity. Those who have an irrational phobia for spiders or snakes will feel specially strong revulsion when they are used as emblems of Clytemnestra's treacherous wickedness (*Agamemnon* 1492, 1516, *Libation-bearers* 249, 994), and when the chorus in *Suppliant Women* 887 describe the approaching enemy as a spider 'advancing step by step, a dream, a black dream'. (How nightmarish and at the same time accurately observed is that 'step by step' – the characteristic dart forward and pause of a stalking spider!) Pity will be strong in the hearts of those who love horses when they hear Cassandra compared to an unbroken filly straining at the bridle with blood and foam on its mouth (*Agamemnon* 1066–7). Metaphors and similes from storms at sea may be hardly more than literary ornaments to someone living in central Europe or America, but they would remind seafaring Athenians of actual shipwrecks and drowning. 'He jests at scars that never felt a wound.'

There is a distinction to be made here. Every adult, ancient or modern, is likely to have similar feelings in response to natural phenomena and everyday experiences such as light, darkness, heat, cold, rain, dew, metal, the sun, the moon, sleeping, singing, dancing, sensations of colour, shape, smell, taste and touch, and so on. (Many of these are ambivalent: fire warms or destroys, water refreshes or drowns.) But everyone will not feel with equal intensity about other symbolical images in tragedy – wolves for silent treachery, nightingales for melodious grief, bulls for clumsy rage or brutal violence, doves for flocking panic, hares for pitiful helplessness, birds robbed of their nestlings for desolate grief, a barnyard cock strutting among his hens for petty pride – all from Aeschylus (and discussed in detail elsewhere) and all immediately appreciable by the Athenians who lived so close to the country. For modern citizens of megalopolis living in the age of machinery many of them are at best little more than museum exhibits. And some others need a lengthy footnote before they become meaningful in our minds or emotive in our hearts because they are based on obsolete customs. The symbolism of a torch race, for example, which underlies Clytemnestra's beacon speech in *Agamemnon*, would evoke feelings of excitement and festivity among Athenians used to civic ceremonies of that kind, feelings that become explicit in the rejoicings in the torchlight procession at the end of *Eumenides*. It is more likely to remind us of an electrical black-out. Unless we make allowances for the emotional as well as for the sociological differences in matters of this kind we shall miss a good deal in the imagery of Greek poetry.

Something else needs also to be kept in mind here – the fact that emotional reaction to symbolism can result from literary, artistic, and religious antecedents as well as from personal experience. Athenians had never seen a Gorgon or any of the monsters that Aeschylus was so fond of introducing into his plays – no more than we have seen a devil or a unicorn. But when the traditional doctrine has been strong the imaginary terrors can be worse than fears of any material object. Symbolism based on lions is common in Greek tragedy, especially in the *Oresteia* where it is heraldically linked with the Atreidai. Though few if any Athenians would ever have seen a lion, the vividly described lions of the Homeric poems and the lively lions of orientalizing art must have created a strong image in the minds of educated audiences. And, for another stock figure of poetic imagery, the nightingale, even if some umbratile, agora-haunting Athenian had never heard one sing, he would remember its appearance in early poetry and in the myth of Procne and Tereus. Keats had never seen a little seaside Greek town such as he evoked so vividly in his *Ode on a Grecian Urn*, nor had Yeats ever sailed to Byzantium.

Several of the symbols mentioned in the previous paragraphs might profitably be explored in terms of modern psychology, especially the snake, the bull, and the spider. But that path – or minotaur-haunted labyrinth – of speculation will be avoided here where we are chiefly concerned with the classical Greek attitudes to emotionalism. The ancient Greek interpreters of dreams speculated about symbolism in less subtle ways, to judge from the copious, but rather banal, information provided by Artemidoros in his *Interpretations of Dreams* (*Oneirokritiká*). (Though he wrote in the second century AD he probably reproduced material going back to the time of the major tragedians.) To dream of a net, he says, means danger and stealthy attacks (Hercher 98, 22 and 208, 5). A raven means adultery, theft, or death (113, 15; 222, 19–23), which is very apt for the chorus's metaphor for Clytemnestra as she stands over the corpse of her cuckolded husband in *Agamemnon* 1473. (But in Aeschylus' *Suppliant Women* 751 the raven embodies a threat of rape to the virgin Danaids.) Spiders portend evil in general (234, 17–18); serpents, sickness or an enemy (106, 17–18); bulls, unusual danger (102, 3 ff.); 'sea-dyed' fabrics (i.e. in the colour scale from purple to red), death (70, 11–12); torches at night, agreeable love-affairs (96, 11–12) and so, too, lamps (67, 14–15). One of Artemidoros' interpretations has relevance for Clytemnestra's dream (*Libation-bearers* 523–33) in which she suckles a snake: if a man dreams of a woman carrying a 'creeping animal' (*herpetón*) in her bosom it means that his wife has committed adultery with his enemy. To dream about Hephaistos symbolizes 'hidden things' particularly adultery (142, 30), since his wife, Aphrodite, committed adultery with Ares. Is it only a coincidence, then, that Aeschylus makes Clytemnestra name Hephaistos at the beginning of her speech about the beacons in *Agamemnon* 281? More will be said about some of these symbols in chapter 9.

Clytemnestra's dream of suckling a snake exemplifies a kind of imagery that deserves the epithet 'sick' as used in contemporary descriptions of humour. In it the emotions are shown as in a diabolical mirror in which the natural order is tainted and distorted. (One might call it sadistic; but in tragedy it has no overt sexual aspects.) The most striking example comes in Clytemnestra's gloating description of how she murdered the King (*Agamemnon* 1385–92). She says that when the sharp spurts of blood from the wounded body fell on her in 'a dark and murderous dew' she rejoiced 'no less than the sown cornfields rejoice at the heavensent brightness (of the dew) at the time when the ear is in its birth-pangs'. Does any passage in literature offer a more concentrated piece of perverted symbolism than that? The joy that the happy cornfields feel in a parched land when the fructifying, gentle moisture falls on them is transformed into a Black Mass of exultant vengeance – dark blood for glistening dew, lethal wounds for life-giving birth pangs, a screaming victim instead of rich cornlands, hate and revenge instead of a heavensent boon – and this from the mouth of the woman who had recently compared her husband's return to 'a stream of water to a thirsty traveller' (901)! A briefer, but equally ghastly, expression of evil perversion comes in *Eumenides* 253 when the Erinyes say 'The smell of blood laughs out at me.'

In these perverse metaphors the characters betray themselves. In others the evil of their natures is explicitly described by observers in terms of traditional monstrosities. Ion thinks of Creousa as a viper or dragon (*Ion* 1262–5). Cassandra (1232–6) compares Clytemnestra to 'a hateful biting beast, an amphisbaina, a kind of Scylla dwelling among rocks, a destruction to sailors, a raging mother of Hades breathing out truceless war-spirit'. The reference to Scylla recurs in Jason's denunciation of Medea (1342–3) – 'a lioness, not a woman, having a more savage nature than Etruscan Scylla'. If, as is not improbable, Athenian children were often terrified by Homer's vivid description in *Odyssey* 12, 85–100, of Scylla with her twelve hanging legs and six hideous heads on long necks, and her sharklike triple rows of thickset teeth, who darted out of her cave on the cliffs and snatched sailors from their ships, then when her name was used in tragedy an echo of a childish terror might still disturb even adult Greeks, like references in comedy to such bogies as Lamia, Mormo (alarming name), Ephialtes, Epialos and Empousa. Homer's description of how Odysseus had helplessly to watch six of his companions being dragged up by the monster into her cave, calling on him and stretching out their hands to him in vain – 'the most pitiful thing that I saw in all my sufferings' – would indelibly affect a child's imagination, like descriptions of the wolf in *Little Red Riding Hood* or the ogre in *Jack and the Beanstalk*. A dramatist can subtly exploit these infantile terrors that lurk in the sub-conscious.

To return to imagery of perverted nature: it is used differently when the chorus in *Medea* 410, having heard Medea's masculine resolve to kill her enemies, exclaim 'Now the currents of the holy rivers flow upwards', and when Ajax after his return to sanity cries out (394–6), 'Oh the darkness is now the light for me, the shades of Hades are now my brightest gleam.' Here the sense of perverted nature is externalized and generalized to express a pervading sense of *tarachē*. The *terra firma* of the natural order has suffered a seismic shock in the hearts of the victims or witnesses of the tragic events, and for a moment they are totally disorientated.

It is in a tragedian's interests to make emotions as concrete as possible in his audience's hearts and minds. He can do this very effectively by personifying them. Grief has 'a bite that reaches to the heart' in *Agamemnon* 791–2. It wears a black robe and is lacerated by anxiety in *Persians* 115–16 and 161. Fear makes the heart dance (*Libation-bearers* 167) and 'expectation of fear' can parade through a house (*Agamemnon* 1434). The anger of Oedipus 'sits close by, with dry, unweeping eyes' (or perhaps 'besets my dry eyes') as his son goes out to fight his brother in *Seven against Thebes* 695–6. Sorrow eats the heart in *Agamemnon* 103. Emotions of various kinds 'seize' or 'tear' people. Perhaps some vestiges of the early Greek belief that the emotions were daemonic energies may survive in these, at least in the time of Aeschylus. But they seem mainly to be the result of imaginative visualization. (The fact that the earliest texts were written entirely in capital letters makes it difficult at times to identify a personification.)

Symbols synthesize vague associations and feelings for emotional effect. Dramatic irony, a much studied topic, works differently. Its range is restricted and it is mainly rational and analytical. The hearer, if he is aware of how the tragic story will end, sees that a statement can be interpreted in a way that the speaker does not realize. Cold-hearted people will think 'Silly fool', mildly sympathetic people, 'Poor fool', and warm-hearted people, 'Poor creature' or more generally in Cassandra's words 'Alas for human efforts' (*philanthrōpía*). Even at its strongest, irony is, and probably was, unlikely to 'fill the seats with weeping multitudes'. There is usually an element of cool Olympian detachment in it, like the mood of Gray in his *Ode on a Distant Prospect of Eton College* –

> Alas! regardless of their doom,
> The little victims play.

Yet pity may grow strong as one watches Oedipus contriving unawares his own doom and hears him use words that are as double-edged as his deeds – pity for a fellow human being caught in what Aeschylus called 'the great net of Ate'

(*Agamemnon* 360–1) – and the more one struggles against that net the tighter the meshes bind.

This kind of irony – 'irony of fate' – is expressed mainly in a character's deeds. He thinks he is moving towards salvation: in fact he is constructing his own destruction. But it is generally accompanied, as so well illustrated in *King Oedipus*, by verbal irony. Sophocles, the most emotionally detached of the three tragedians, is the acknowledged master of this technique, as the scholia to his plays frequently illustrate. (For example the scholiast on *King Oedipus* 236ff. remarks 'The statement evokes great pity because he is accusing himself without knowing it', and on 246ff. 'Unawares he curses himself . . . and as a result the statement is very pathetic', and on 928 'The poet has put in an amphiboly here, which gives pleasure to the hearer'.) But Euripides also uses verbal irony with fully Sophoclean skill at times. In the scene before Pentheus goes to his ghastly *sparagmós* we hear the following dialogue (*Bacchai* 965–70):

> *Dionysos* I shall go as your protective escort, but another will bring you back.
> *Pentheus* Yes – my mother.
> *Dionysos* And you will be clearly seen by all.
> *Pentheus* That's what I'm going for.
> *Dionysos* You will be carried back. . . .
> *Pentheus* You're promising me luxury.
> *Dionysos* In your mother's arms.
> *Pentheus* You're spoiling me with indulgence.
> *Dionysos* Yes, indulgence of a kind.
> *Pentheus* Indeed I'm getting what I deserve.

Like time-bombs set to explode in a few minutes of theatrical time, every phrase here is explosive. Pentheus as represented by his severed head will indeed be carried back triumphantly in his mother's arms, and he will indeed get what he deserves from Dionysos' point of view.

To turn now to the question of emotional power in the structure of drama, the 'plot'. Most discussions of this topic dwell on Aristotle's analysis in terms of 'recognitions' (*anagnōriseis*) and 'reversals' (*peripéteiai*), and *páthē*. There is uncertainty about what he means by this last term in *Poetics* 1452b 10 since it cannot mean 'emotions' in this context. It seems best to take it as indicating such moments of suffering shown on scene as the deaths of Alcestis and Hippolytos and the impaling of Prometheus. Though Aristotle insists that their ultimate purpose is to evoke pity and fear, in fact he dwells mostly on their intellectual aspects – causal connections, logic and surprise. He treats tragedy here, as if it were a series of statements and demonstrations, despite the fact that elsewhere he emphasizes the basic difference between mimesis and actuality. This emphasis on the intellectual aspects reflects Aristotle's own personal inclinations. As a scientist and logician he was happier in dealing with matters of reason – identifications, changes of direction in the reversals and describable types of action – rather than with vaguer matters of feeling.

From the emotional point of view the structural effects of Greek tragedy can perhaps be better understood by considering them in terms of a musical composition in which feelings are orchestrated and arranged, rather than in terms of events. Like the great instrumental and choral compositions of Bach, Mozart and Beethoven, the tragic dramas succeed by means of crescendos and diminuendos, accelerandos and rallentandos, scherzo movements and maestoso movements, recurrent motifs and ingenious variations. This will be exemplified more fully in the next chapter by analysing a single masterpiece, 'movement' by 'movement' as in a symphony. Only some general principles will be noticed here.

The familiar overall pattern is generally this: preparation for the tragic event, then (usually about two-thirds of the way through the play) description of the catastrophe, then the consequences of the catastrophe. For the audience this means suspense, distress, grief. But there are many variations. *Eumenides, Oedipus at Colonos, Philoctetes,* Sophocles' *Electra, Helen, Iphigeneia among the Tauri,* and *Alcestis* have the happy ending that Aristotle depreciates as being weak in causing pity and fear. So far as emotionalism *per se* is concerned one might argue that joy and happiness are as valid as sorrow and grief. But by common consent the more sorrowful emotions are generally the strongest. The tragic *Iliad* is more deeply moving than the *Odyssey* with its happy ending.

Tragedies also vary in the importance of a preceding *páthos*. In *Persians, Seven, Agamemnon, Prometheus, King Oedipus, Ajax, Trojan Women* and *Hecuba*, an earlier catastrophe is very much in the author's and the audience's minds, while others like *Medea* and *Alcestis* are more independent. Some, like the continuous symphonies of Schumann and Sibelius, run on steadily without marked changes of mood, notably *Persians, Seven* and *Medea* (except for the Aigeus episode), in contrast with *Agamemnon, Ajax* and *Women of Trachis* where different feelings alternate.

Sophocles is best at achieving a *scherzo* effect with outbursts of gladness after grief and gloom, as in the tremendous burst of ecstatic joy by the chorus in *Ajax* 693–718. The same technique is used almost as effectively in *Women of Trachis* and *Oedipus at Colonos*. The technique in *Agamemnon* is different. Onwards from the Watchman's opening speech the feelings of joy at the end of the war are overshadowed and muted by a lurking fear of what is going to happen soon in Argos, and this *chiaroscuro* continues until the end of the trilogy.

Another way of alternating emotions is to introduce touches of almost comic realism as when the Nurse in *Libation-bearers* 748–60 describes her troubles with Orestes as a baby, and in the more complex 'sick' comedy of dressing Pentheus, that misogynist, in feminine clothes in *Bacchai* 912ff. Perhaps, too, the rustic characters in *King Oedipus* and Euripides' *Electra* and the Watchman in *Agamemnon* had some comic features. But there is nothing in Greek tragedy to equal the scenes of broad comedy that Shakespeare interspersed in his tragedies.

Nor are there any Shakespearian sub-plots. On the other hand there are many cases of what might be called sub-emotions by which the main subject of pity and fear is supported by subsidiary comparisons. This is a regular feature

of the choric songs. Its most direct method is to compare the
hero or heroine's fate with that of others famous in tragic
myths. Or else a subsidiary character, like Io in *Prometheus*,
augments the pitifulness of the general situation. Perhaps
Aeschylus originally intended Cassandra's role in *Agamemnon*
to be merely subsidiary, but, like Mercutio in *Romeo and
Juliet*, she grew in his imagination into one of the most
memorably pitiful characters in European drama. Another
kind of sub-emotion has already been noticed in the imagery of
suffering animals. In *Agamemnon* our faculty for pity is first
aroused by the brief glimpse of the trembling pregnant hare
being eaten by the eagles, then it is more strongly evoked in the
descriptions of Menelaos, and the grief of the bereaved
Argives. Ultimately these variations on the theme of pity reach
a climax in the scenes with Cassandra and after Agamemnon's
death.

Anger is similarly orchestrated in *Ajax*. First we have the
anger of Ajax, then Teucer's anger (with a passing reference in
1017 to the irascibility of their father Telamon), and finally –
with a lowering of the heroic level – the mean-spirited anger of
Menelaos and Agamemnon. Angry hate operates in much the
same way in *Medea*, and in both plays the prevailing sombre
mood is relieved by moments of patriotic feeling (*philopatría*).
In *Ajax* the sailors yearn for their native Salamis (596ff.), and in
Medea the chorus of Corinthian women praise Athens in the
famous apostrophe to the 'happy children of Erectheus . . .
ever delicately moving through their most clear and shining
air'. These descriptions of familiar localities would have had
something like the effect of the direct addresses to the audience
in Greek comedy. They would strengthen the *rapport* between
the choruses and the listening Athenians as well as warming
patriotic feelings.

The most fearful and pitiful change of atmosphere in Greek
tragedy is, of course, the major catastrophe, the sudden move
from happiness and prosperity to grief and deprivation. Often
it comes abruptly with death-cries or with a messenger's
announcement. At other times it approaches gradually like a

spectre in a nightmare, most brilliantly in *King Oedipus*. In *Bacchai* 810 one syllable marks the turning-point. Up to that moment Dionysos has been treating the youthful intransigent Pentheus with tolerant patience. But now after further hybris from the King he decides to 'turn on the heat'. Unlike Hitler at a fateful moment in European history, Dionysos does not proclaim 'My patience is at an end.' Instead all he utters is *â*, prolonged for the length of a whole line and pronounced with the rising-falling inflection indicated by the circumflex accent (not the *á* of surprise or pain). Enuciated with all the tonal skill of a practised actor it must have been blood-curdling. From that moment onwards Pentheus is doomed, though Euripides delays the catastrophe with the sardonic episode in which Pentheus is dressed in feminine clothes and mocked by Dionysos.

Aristotle does not suggest a *peripéteia* of emotions as distinct from a *peripéteia* of action. But a permanent charge in the emotional atmosphere – as distinct from brief alternations of grief and joy – occurs in several tragedies. In the last scene of *Agamemnon* the mainly passive reactions of the chorus change to a mood of defiance and revenge. In *Eumenides* the menacing cloud of fear is dispelled by the radiant light of deliverance and joy. In *Antigone* hatred of Creon's tyranny gives way to compassion for him when bereaved of son and wife. And most tragedies, whatever their earlier prevailing emotions are, end in *éleos*.

Euripides handles this kind of *peripéteia* with particular skill in *Bacchai*. In the first three-quarters of the play we are clearly intended to dislike Pentheus as a bullying puritan, and to sympathize with the debonair Dionysos. But our feelings must change when the Messenger (1115ff.) describes how the young King died, how he touched his mother's cheek and begged her to spare him despite the mistakes he has made, unaware that she is totally under the influence of the angry god:

But he did not persuade her. Then she taking in her arms [terrible irony of phrase] his left hand, and standing on the

ribs of the wretched man, wrenched off his shoulder. . . .
And her sister set to work on the other side, rending his
flesh. . . . There was clamour everywhere – his groans,
their triumph-cries. One woman carried off an elbow,
another a foot still in its boot. His flanks were stripped to
the bone as they tore him apart. With hands all smeared
with blood they tossed the flesh of Pentheus to each other,
like playing with a ball.

Even in prose the appalling horror of this scene with its
comparison to an innocent game (like Nausicaä's on the sea-
coast of Phaeacia) cannot fail to turn us against Dionysos and
towards the hapless Pentheus. Perhaps even for a moment we
feel repulsion towards his mother as well. But this is quickly
dispelled by the extreme pathos of the following scene when
she realizes what she has done. In the end she even dares to tell
Dionysos that he has gone too far in his revenge – 'Gods should
not be like mortals in their angry passions' (*orgás* 1346–8).

The moral and theological implications of this reversal have
been widely debated. Emotionally there is no problem.
Euripides has extended the technique of emotional *peripéteia*
to its limit with great dramatic success. From the point of view
of literary artistry this is all that matters.

Another type of structuring that can contribute strongly to
emotionalism is not noticed by the ancient literary critics – the
structuring of imagery as distinct from action. Though
Sophocles and Euripides use this technique effectively at times
(as with the sickness theme in *King Oedipus*), Aeschylus is its
supreme exponent. His usual method is to introduce a
symbolic image *pianissimo* early in a play and then to let it grow
to a *fortissimo* either by giving it a more emphatic form or else
by making it emerge as an actuality (like the net motif in
Agamemnon, as will be noticed in the next chapter). This
technique is best exemplified in *Seven against Thebes* where
the image of a ship in a storm combined with Alcaeus' allegory
of the Ship of State in distress acts as a strong *leit motiv*
throughout the main part of the play. It recurs explicitly no less

than thirteen times, and yet it is not tediously obtrusive. It begins with two direct metaphors identifying Eteocles' preparations to resist attack with naval precautions (32, 62–4). The idea of the storm is strengthened in 114–15 when the chorus sings 'A slanting-crested wave plashes around the city of our menfolk, urged on by the blasts of war.' From then on there are many references to noise, as noticed in chapter 4, and the noise of the imaginary storm is modulated into the actual noises of the enemies' horses and chariots (203–10). After an interval (unless the repeated references to *púrgoi* carry a nautical association) the metaphor emerges quietly again when the boasting of one of the attackers is called 'wave-surging words' (443), and it continues in unemphatic terms in 595, 602–4, and 652. Then in 690–1 the motif changes key. After Eteocles decides to go and fight against his brother it ceases to refer to the danger to Thebes and the fear of the chorus. Now for a moment it expresses grief rather than fear, lamentation rather than cries of panic, while the current of Cocytas the 'River of Wailing' in Hades, takes the place of the sea (690–1). But the image returns in 705–9, 752–62 and 766–71. In 792–802 the hearts of the chorus are raised by the Messenger's announcement that the hostile champions have been killed: 'The city has reached calm weather: it has not foundered under the many shocks of the surge.' But the chorus soon learn that Eteocles has died with his brother, and a flood of grief sweeps over them. They see themselves no longer now as passengers in a storm-tossed ship but as the crew of a grief-laden bark sailing down to Hades (854–60):

> But now, O friends, row down on the breeze of grief,
> Beating your heads with hands, a throbbing stroke
> That rows the bleak and black-sailed bark of grief
> Down Acheron – no festive voyage this –
> To the sunless shore that Phoebus always shuns,
> That all-receiving and all-darkening coast.

No other passage in Greek literature more powerfully expresses the desolate despair of the pagan Greeks in face of what W. E. Henley called 'the horror of the shade'. The brief, bright calm after the storm has turned into a night of sorrow for a lost leader. It would have made a superb ending to the play, and perhaps, as some scholars believe, the play did end there. (If the rest is an addition, the interpolator was skilful enough to maintain the dominant image of a ship in a storm in 992 and in the closing lines.)

Structurally what we have here is a kind of *peripéteia* from the image of a ship of fear to that of a ship of grief. Musically it is like a modulation from a major to a minor key (as probably the music of the accompanying pipe made plain). If we wonder why this powerful emotive technique was used less emphatically in later plays, perhaps an explanation is to be found in tragedy's development from lyrical methods to more strictly dramatic methods in which narrative and exposition were valued more highly than manipulated imagery and symbolism, and logical structure displaced musical structure, until at the end of the fifth century Melpomene after a long struggle with sophists and rhetoricians finally abandoned her home in Athens. Yet, like Cleopatra just before her death, she had a last moment of brilliance and greatness in the lyricism of *Bacchai*.

CHAPTER NINE

The tragic emotions in the *Oresteia*

In this chapter it is proposed to illustrate how the emotive methods already described are used cumulatively and on a grand scale by a master poet. The form adopted will be that of a running commentary focused on the expression and arousal of emotions in *Agamemnon*, together with some brief remarks on the rest of the trilogy. The editions to which I am chiefly indebted are those of Denniston and Page, Fraenkel, Groeneboom, Rose, Thomson and Headlam, and also Lloyd-Jones's commentary on his translation (see my bibliography). These are referred to by their authors' initials. When words are italicized, including Greek terms, it means that they are discussed elsewhere, as indicated in the index. Readers would do well to have the Greek text or a translation with them for reference.

1–39 Here in the lively speech of the Watchman Aeschylus, like a musician in the overture to a long and elaborate composition, briefly and for the most part unobtrusively introduces most of the trilogy's emotional themes. Fear is most strongly presented. Personified in 14, and indicated by *disturbed syntax* in 12–15, it then yields to grief and groaning for the present state of affairs in the royal house at Argos. These unhappy feelings are momentarily banished by joy at the appearance of the long-awaited beacon and by the anticipated pleasures both of winning a reward for being the first to announce the good news and of welcoming the King on his return (*philía*). The sense of fear returns in the last lines, all the more ominously by being undefined as to its source. The final mood is that of the opening scenes in *Hamlet*: there's something so rotten – and fearful – in the State of Argos that even this bluff watchman does not dare to speak freely.

Other remarks of his prepare the ground for emotional responses later in the play. The description of the Queen as having a heart that combines the hopefulness of a woman with the purposefulness of a man very quietly introduces the motif of *perverted nature* and *monstrosity*, which will swell to terrifying proportions. The symbolism of light (for joy) and darkness (for sorrow) will recur with many variations – dawn, torches, lamps, stars, the sun, shining justice and much else – all through the trilogy and will help to glorify its triumphant *finale*. The house, the accursed House of the Atreidai that stands like a silent character in the background of the action and looms up with terrible menace before the exits of Agamemnon and Cassandra, is mentioned five times (see further on 958–74). It is almost given a voice in 37–8.

We have here, too, a miniature exploitation of the technique of alternating emotions: suspense, fear, joy (perhaps visually expressed by a few dance steps at 31 as well as by the cries of *ioú, ioú* in 25), and finally fear again. An audience primarily interested in the character of the Watchman and the events he describes would hardly be conscious of these emotional sequences (see further in chapter 9), but like a melody played quietly in the bass while the treble tune is kept dominant, they prepare the way for crescendos to come. The last warning 'I speak to those who undestand' might just be Aeschylus himself telling his audience to expect cryptic meanings in what follows: cf. 144–5, 615–16.

40–71 New emotions are mentioned briefly here – anger on the part of the Atreidai and the gods, pity for the robbed birds, *érōs* on the part of Helen 'the woman of many men (or husbands)' in 62. The note of grief at a disturbed home in 18–19 is re-echoed in the grief of the 'eagles' (hardly vultures in this regal context) for their robbed nest.

78–82 The *cliché* of the pitiable condition of *old age* is exploited emphatically in these lines. The chorus for a moment provide a third object of pity after the robbed birds and (implicitly) the limb-weary warriors at Troy in 63–7.

92–6 A different kind of torch, symbolizing thanksgiving, is lit. These torches are 'medicined by gentle, undeceitful persuasions of royal oilcake from the innermost part of the house'. This is strange suggestive language, possibly in preparation for the deeper symbolism of the torches to emerge later (see on 281). The word for the innermost part of the house here, *mukhós*, is used by Homer in his reference to Aigisthos' seduction of Clytemnestra in *Odyssey* 3, 263.

99–103 The motif of anxiety becomes emphatic. The text of 103 is corrupt, but something like 'insatiable worry and spirit-consuming grief of heart' seems to be indicated. This implies more than concern about the significance of the sudden sacrifices and illuminations. It expresses a deep-seated uneasiness of a general kind. Cf. on 160–83.

104–39 *Significant rhythm*: after the conventional iambics and anapaests of the preceding passages the dactylic hexameters and subsequent sporadic dactyls strike a chord which combines heroic *êthos* with oracular overtones, the first being apt for the picture of Achaean warlords on the march and the second preparing the way for the omen of the eagles and its interpretation. Lines 107, 116 and 126 can be scanned as a combination of a *dochmiac*, the metre of tension and strain, with dactyls.

In 119ff. a minor reversal in emotional direction occurs. The pitiful birds of 49–54 are replaced by birds which are emblems of savage cruelty: instead of losing their own young they are now destroyers of another creature's offspring (just as the Atreidai who were shown as being deprived of their nestling, Helen, in 60–2, will turn into murderers of another nestling, Iphigeneia, in 228–47). Artemis' reaction to the slaughter of the hare and leverets moves in two directions – pity (*oîktos*, 134, first specifically named here) for the hare and both *phthónos* and loathing (*stúgos*) towards the eagles (134, 137). The *refrain* in 121 begins as a lament for the slaughter of the animals and for the wrath of Artemis, but continues in 139 and 159 as a preparation for the more terrible child-slaughter that is to come.

149–59 After a repetition of the motif of waiting (*suspense*: cf. 1–2) the chorus introduces a tremendous personification of *Anger* in its most heavily charged form (*mênis*) – 'Fearsome wrath that abides and springs up again and controls the house (*oikonómos*), deceives and remembers and brings vengeance for children.' (A strong alliteration of *m* and *n* creates an aural climax for the word *mênis*, and the slowing of the rhythm at the words for 'remember' and 'anger' adds emphasis.) In fact this might almost be a description of Clytemnestra, as *oikonómos* strongly hints, since this word could also mean 'house-keeper'. She indeed embodies the abiding wrath of the house of Atreus, as the chorus partly recognise in 1507–12. The harsh resonance of the verb describing Calchas' tone of voice as he uttered these ominous words – *apéklanxen* – both embodies the actual sound and suggests a *nomen omen* for the name, *Kálkhas*. Cf. on 201.

160–83 Mainly unemotional. But, as DP suggests, the reference to 'this vain burden of anxiety' may refer to the chorus's general uneasiness and not exclusively to their theological problems. In the phrase 'Instead of sleep the travail (*pónos*) of remembered woe drips out in front of the heart' we have an ominous echo of the Watchman's complaint about his inability to sleep (through fear in his case). If we read *bíaios* agreeing with *cháris* we have a *noxymoron* – 'forcible benevolence' – to express *tarachḗ*. This quiet meditative passage provides a *calm before the storm* in preparation for the first major emotional scene (described, not acted) in the play.

184–98 *Tarachḗ* also possesses Agamemnon. It is symbolized in the to-and-fro currents int he straits at Aulis – the notorious Euripos whose irregular tides are said to have baffled even

Aristotle. The motif of weary waiting is stressed again in 194–8. As Ll-J observes, the syncopated iambics (192ff.) after the previous trochees effectively express the frustration of the delay. He also believes that the choriambics of 199ff. express the violent reaction of the princes to the prophet's words.

200–4 'The prophet clanged out (*éklanxen*) . . .': again both the name and the harshly ringing voice of the prophet are embodied in the verb, but what he actually said is left to our imagination. We are told only its consequences, the tears of the Atreidai and the ensuing sacrifice. The *gesture* of the Atreidai, striking the ground with their staffs, seems to indicate that their grief is mixed with anger (cf. *Iliad* 1, 245 and *Odyssey* 2, 80).

1–204 Recapitulation. It may be well here to assess how skilfully Aeschylus in preparation for the Iphigeneia scene has gradually raised the emotional temperature – that is, the emotional temperature of us, the audience, not just of the people in the play. At the outset we probably felt some sympathetic vibrations of fear – and of momentary joy – with the Watchman, engaging character that he was. But they were hardly more than slight forebodings, though the words that the chorus sang in 98–103 strengthened them. Our compassion has been mildly appealed to in the references to the robbed birds, to the warriors wearily battling at Troy, and to the slaughtered hare and leverets, as well as by the weariness of the Watchman at his long vigil. If we had been present at a performance with a powerful actor playing Clytemnestra we might have felt a *frisson* of fear from the mere sight of her as she moved silently across the scene at 83ff., ignoring the chorus's deferential questions (as I believe she must despite strong arguments against her entrance here). The other emotions mentioned – anger, *phthónos*, grief and *taraché* – have had only a slight impact as yet.

Down to 104 Aeschylus has not used any of the strong emotive techniques (described in chapter 7) in his diction. He has been content to refer to the various emotions for the most part in cool language and conventional rhythms. But when the dactyls and dochmiacs begin to sound in 104ff. they mark an *accelerando* for our pulse-beats. The introduction of a lamentatory prayer in 121 and its double repetition as a refrain – with its traditionally emotive evocation of *Linos* – marks a further increase in emotive stimulus. The same purpose is achieved by the accumulation of intensive compound epithets, by the strong alliteration and assonance in 154–6, and by the personification of Wrath in 155. The first emotional gestures that are clearly indicated come in 202–3 when we are told that the Atreidai wept for grief and struck the ground in anger. All this, together with the cumulative effect of the repeated emotional motifs, would prepare us – unconsciously, perhaps, if we were an audience in a theatre seeing the play for the first time – for the appalling scene that is to come, a scene which, if imposed on us in cold blood, might cause us to feel *stúgos* and *ékplēxis* rather than compassionate grief.

205–17 Agamemnon is still in a state of *tarachḗ*. On the one hand, he is affected by *storgḗ* for his daughter, 'the delight of his home', and by the horror of 'polluting a father's hands with streams from the slaughter of a virgin'. On the other, there is the duty of loyalty to the army whose leader he is. His decision to yield to the second motive is expressed in strange terms 'because it is right to desire virginal blood with over-angry anger' – or, if *orgḗ* here has its more general meaning of swelling passion, we should translate (with F) 'with over-passionate passion'. Editors for centuries, as F observes, have objected to 'this intolerable expression' with its *tautology* and *hyperbole*. But these, as we have seen, are normal in highly emotional speech, and the violence of the sentiment is psychologically appropriate. Agamemnon's decision is not the result of rationally weighing the arguments for and against the sacrifice. It is an emotional conflict between the *storgḗ* of a father and the blood-lust of angry warriors (cf. 48 and 230) who will strike down whatever stands in the way of their revenge, even an innocent girl. Agamemnon uses the strongest possible term, *thémis* for the truly monstrous assertion that it is right and lawful to passionately desire the blood of a virgin (this word is used twice to emphasize the pity of an *unmarried girl's* early death). He has to wrench himself away from moral standards as well as from personal affection if he is to commit this appalling deed. That is why he uses such strong language in making his decision. But we must feel a flicker of compassion for him when he adds the pathetically futile prayer, 'May it be well' (echoing the earlier refrain).

218–27 The chorus have no doubt about the nature of this decision which is metaphorically identified with a change of wind (so, too, less emphatically in 187) – a typical Aeschylean blending of actuality and symbolism. Agamemnon, they sing, was now 'blowing an impious, impure, unholy wind-change of heart-and-mind' (*phrēn*), and 'from then he changed his thinking-and-feeling (*phroneîn*) towards the utterly reckless deed'. (Translators tend to emphasize the mental process of decision-making here, but Aeschylus keeps the emotional element in mind by using *phrēn*.) With a touch of *philanthrōpía* the chorus reflect that his recklessness is a regularly observable phenomenon once a person is overcome by psychological derangement.

228–47 This passage brilliantly exemplifies the ability of the Greek lyric poets to paint a heart-rending scene in a brief compass. Though the description of Iphigeneia's death lasts only for twenty lines its emotional impact is as powerful as any scene in Greek tragedy, and in performance it had the advantage over a messenger's description of a catastrophe of being supported by music and dancing. It incorporates several favourite *éleoi* – the death of an innocent marriageable girl (like Polyxena and Macaria), the agony of a parent compelled not only to witness but to cause his child's death (like Medea), and the contrast between present disaster and former *happiness*.

If 239 – literally 'pouring to the ground dyes of saffron' – means 'letting fall to the ground her saffron raiment' in the sense of disrobing herself so as to stand naked before what Tennyson in his brilliant re-enactment of the scene in *A Dream of Fair Women* calls 'the stern, black-bearded kings with wolfish eyes', then we have a startling and unique emotional gesture. Iphigeneia in a last desperate effort to soften the hearts of the angry war-lords lets her robe fall to the ground and stands before them totally naked, hoping that the sheer helplessness and innocence of her young body will move them to pity. She cannot speak because her 'fair-prowed mouth' has been gagged as Agamemnon ordered. (The second element in the adjective is not 'meaningless' as DP says: it is there to remind us of the ships that await release.) So she can only 'strike each one of the sacrificers with a pity-seeking dart (*oxymoron*) from her eye' and let her whole body speak, 'standing out clear to see as in a picture' (242). (One may think, in modern terms, of Botticelli's *Birth of Venus*.) F, who supports the view that Iphigeneia disrobes herself (so, too, HT, R, and G), compassionately comments, 'In the general picture of her appearance, the element of *phíloikton* rises to a level that almost unnerves one'. (He contrasts 'the simple grandeur' of this scene with the ostentatious care for decorum shown by Polyxena in *Hecuba* 558–70.)

If this interpretation is accepted, the order of events would be this: Agamemnon orders the attendants to take his daughter and raise her over the altar like an animal for sacrifice 'wrapped in her clothes and drooping forward (as he anticipates) in all her spirit'. (The alliteration and word-order in 134 hardly allow one to take *pantì thumôi* as referring to the attendants, though F does so.) Agamemnon also orders them first to gag her to prevent possible words of ill omen. But after they have gagged her and before they seize her Iphigeneia slips off her robe and lets her eyes and her body make a last appeal – the appeal of helpless, innocent, beautiful young womanhood. (The scholiast emphasizes the element of beauty in the phrase 'as in a picture', rightly, I think, cf. *Hecuba* 560–1.) Our last glimpse of Iphigeneia, then, will not be that of an overwhelmed, drooping victim but of a royal princess of the heroic age (like

Cassandra) making one last desperate, but not ignoble, bid for her life.

But this order of events and the view that 'pouring to the ground dyes of saffron' means disrobing herself have been strongly contested (see e.g. HT, Lloyd-Jones in *CR* 66 (1952) 132–5, Lebeck 81–2, J. T. Hooker in *Agon* 2 (1968) 59–65). Undeniably there are strong, but not decisive, arguments against it. (Maas's suggestion in *CQ* 45 (1951) 44, that a vase-painting showing Iphigeneia fully clothed during the scarifice was Aeschylus' model here is only a very remote possibility: for Timanthes' version see chapter 7.)

In *dubia* of this kind, where the arguments are strong on both sides and reputable scholars radically disagree, our best guide may be something similar to the maxim of textual critics in similar circumstances – instead of *difficilior lectio potior*, *audacior sententia potior*. If we adopt the more daring inter-pretation – more daring since complete disrobement of this kind is unparalleled in Greek literature, though Polyxena bares her body to the navel and other heroines, as we have seen, bare their breasts in appeals – we can take it as a typically Aeschylean touch of *ékplēxis*. The shock is only momentary and not enough to numb our feelings of pity.

It seems likely that the reference to saffron carries *colour symbolism*, but its primary relevance is widely disputed. Various suggestions are: a royal colour for a princess; a nuptial colour to suggest the pathos of dying unmarried; a cult colour for Artemis; a festive colour; the colour of blood; the colour of tears (see the editors and also Goheen (1955) 115–26, Lebeck 80–91, N.B. Booth in *Eranos* 77 (1972) 85–95). The most likely intention, perhaps, is to sustain the imagery of what Lebeck calls 'the endless flow of blood' in the trilogy, anticipating the blood-coloured tapestries on which Agamemnon will walk to his death and the blood-coloured garment that Orestes displays in *Libation-bearers*.

In 242–6 Aeschylus increases the pitifulness by a 'flash-back' to the happy days before the declaration of war when Iphigeneia charmed the same ruthless commanders by singing to them 'lovingly' after dinners in her 'loving' father's palace (*phílos, phílou* and cf. *philoíktōi* in 241). All such love is far from her now. The poignant scene, however, is startlingly disrupted by a brutal word describing her virginity, *ataúrōtos*, 'unbulled' (245). Editors for the most part have tried to emasculate this expression. F translates it as 'virgin' and quotes Wilamowitz's suggestion that it is perhaps a 'hieratic' term. DP finds it 'extraordinary and apparently brutal', but renders it as 'chaste'. HT says nothing about it, though T translates 'pure and spotless'. R merely compares the metaphor with 1125–6, 'Keep the bull from the cow'. G does not comment on its tone.

The alternative to such palliatives is to accept that Aeschylus intended the term 'unbulled' to be brutal and shocking with the full force that it carries in *Lysistrata* 217 (cf. Eustathius 1183, 20–1, LSJ at *taûros* III, and Henderson 127, 133, 202–3). The bull is an obvious symbol of savage and angry male violence, which is exactly what is causing Iphigeneia's death here, though not in a sexual form. (But modern psychologists might regard the shedding of a virgin's blood as a kind of rape.) Such a symbolism would serve to highlight the innocence and gentleness of this scene-within-a-scene of the girl singing 'with pure voice' (244) at her father's banquets, in contrast with the scene now as she stands gagged among 'the war-loving commanders' (230). The emotional power is strengthened by the *hyperbaton* of the word-order in the full phrase – 'with pure, being unbulled, utterance, her loving father's fortune-bringing (what irony!) paean she lovingly honoured'. A similar use of gross sexual symbolism will be suggested on 1442–7, but there Aeschylus' aim is to evoke disgust towards the speaker and not pity for the victim.

248–57 With masterly artistic control Aeschylus avoids describing the actual killing. If he had not done so he would have reduced the effect of the two main climaxes of pity that are to come. The chorus, deeply moved, take refuge in platitudes.

258–81 This is mostly *êthos*, but two emotions are touched on – *phthónos* in a weak sense (263), and joy expressed in terms of *hyperbole* by Clytemnestra (266) and with glad tears by the chorus (270). The deferential terms of the Coryphaios' address to the Queen and his use of the term *krátos* for her power (cf. 10 and 104 and the character Kratos in *Prometheus*) echo the Watchman's apprehensions. The marked *p* alliteration in 268 expresses 'breathless excitement' (F) at the good news of the capture of Troy. In much of what Clytemnestra says until Agamemnon has been ensnared we must watch out for *allēgoríai*, double-meaning phrases that 'speak to those who understand'. When in 266 she speaks of 'joy beyond expectation', she probably has her own private joy in mind as well as the joy of victory – the joy of knowing that soon she will have her revenge on Agamemnon (as her *Schadenfreude* in 1391–2 suggests).

281–316 Clytemnestra's superbly vivid and imaginative speech about the chain of beacons serves two main purposes, one ethical, the other symbolical. In terms of characterization one feels – and can hardly help admiring – the Queen's energy leaping and pulsating with the flames that are so joyous (287), vigorous (296), exuberant (301), and victory-bringing (314). Her description embodies what the Watchman told us (11) about her 'hopeful heart'. (The Greek word *elpís*, as Verrall observed on 11, can include what we would call imagination.)

Symbolically the already established imagery of torches as emblems of joy becomes prominent here (cf. 21ff. and 88ff.). But there is a further possibility. Hephaistos (281) was notorious in mythology for having been cuckolded by his wife Aphrodite when she committed adultery with Ares, as described in *Odyssey* 8, 267ff. Artemidoros (Hercher, 142, 29–30) says that to dream about Hephaistos foretells adultery. Is this then Aeschylus' first *sotto voce* hint at the Queen's adulterous relationship with Aigisthos? (See further on 609–10.)

320–50 In this equally vivid and imaginative speech on what Clytemnestra imagines is now happening in the captured city we can feel a sense of pity for what both the conquered and the conquerors have been suffering. Then, ominously, she speaks of the risk that lust (*érōs*) for plunder and destruction may cause the destroyers to be destroyed. Even more ominous, in view of Iphigeneia's recently described fate, is her phrase 'the wakeful sufferings of the dead'. Finally when she says 'may the good have the strength to prevail' (the *krátos* motif again) she does not mean what the chorus meant in their refrain and its echo in 255: she means may her own plans succeed, so that she may be the victor in the last lap (314). In all these ambiguous remarks of hers we should remember how Demetrios signalized the use of *allēgoría* to evoke fear.

355–402 The chorus, after a brief, and not very exuberant, expression of thanksgiving – their joy in 270 has been muted by Clytemnestra's ominous remarks – now turn to reflections on crime and punishment. The symbolism of the net is emphatically introduced with two synonyms (358, 361), and the image of light (389) is momentarily perverted to something frightening and baleful.

404–87 With the presentation of Helen to our full attention here (contrast 62) the fourth main emotional theme of the play comes into prominence – *érōs*, with *póthos* and *storgḗ*. The consequence of Helen's yielding to *érōs* is the pitiful *páthos* of Menelaos and the grieving *storgḗ* of the Argive citizens for their dead kinsmen in the Troad. Menelaos' yearning for 'her that is over the ocean' puts into one word in the Greek (*huperpontías*) all the feeling of the folk-song 'My bonny lies over the ocean, My bonny lies over the sea, My bonny lies over the ocean, Oh bring back my bonny to me' (cf. *Persians* 135–9). The double power of Helen's beauty is obliquely expressed: its aesthetic appeal is implied in Menelaos' total loss of appreciation of 'shapely statues' in his palace (such *anorexia aesthetica* is a characteristic feature of this kind of mental and emotional state), while its erotic power is implied in the phrase used by the 'seers of the house (409)' – 'man-(or husband-) loving (cf.

on 856) steps (or traces)'. Menelaos' utter prostration is vividly expressed (with asyndeton) in the phrase 'silence, without honour, without reproach, without belief'. The description of Helen's phantom in the house and of her elusive form 'slipping through his arms' in dreams, presents an unforgettably pitiful picture in a few lines. (For psychological interpretations see Devereux 59–140.)

'These', we are told, 'are the woes at the hearth within the house.' The assonance between the words for 'woes' (*ákhē*) and the word for the empty look in Menelaos' eyes (*akhēniais*) links the two ideas together. But, the chorus continue, there are worse woes in the houses of the citizens of Argos, woes that 'touch the very liver' (432) – grief for the dead Greeks at Troy. This is the grief of *storgē* not *érōs*. There is also an aesthetic element in this grief, as the poignant quatrain in 452–5 records:

> They, in their shapely beauty,
> Near to the Trojan ramparts
> Keep their graves. But the hostile land
> Covers the men who possessed it.

This is an isometric rendering of the rhythms of this quatrain which consists of 2 pherecratics and a glyconic and a pherecratic (or 2 pherecratics and a priapeum), a gentle Aeolic rhythm. The same metrical group has already been used in 381–4, 399–402, 416–19, 433–6, and it will appear once more in 471–3. It constitutes a rhythmical refrain (see F p.186) which isolates and links together the salient themes of the ode – avenging justice, the sin of Paris, the grief of Menelaos, the deaths of Greeks at Troy, their burial far from home, and a prayer to be spared from the cruel victories and defeats of war.

The quatrain quoted from 452–5 is also linked verbally with that describing Menelaos' loss of love for beautiful statues by the repetition of the word for 'shapely' (*eúmorphos*). As editors have noticed, the grief expressed here for citizens killed in a foreign land may echo the feelings of the Athenians in the time of their costly campaign in Egypt. But it also expresses the sadness of all war graves. One may recall Rupert Brooke's lonely tomb on Scyros or the cemeteries of the soldiers who died opposite Troy in Gallipoli in 1915. Here, in a characteristically Greek way, a wry sense of the irony of fate is inserted into the pathos – the possessors are possessed, the victors are vanquished (as Clytemnestra foresaw in 340).

456–74 The *phthónos* (456) aroused among the Argive citizens by the deaths of their relatives 'through another man's wife' turns to angry resentment (*kótos*, smouldering anger) in 456. Worse still, as the chorus's 'anxiety' (460) suggests, the gods and the dark Erinyes may be aroused by all this killing to send 'the man who is lucky without justice' down into darkness. Here as elsewhere several translators, including F, assume that the anxiety is mental not visceral. In fact it is probably both.

475–78 The symbolism of fire is given another twist. The chorus observe that one can interpret a fire-signal wrongly, letting one's heart flare up like a flame and then sink down when the truth is known. And –here Aeschylus is devising further variations on the fire-theme – aren't rumours spread by women like brushwood fires, quickly lit and quickly quenched (if that is how we should take the metaphor in 485)? The fire imagery lingers on in 489–97.

503–86 The Herald renews the note of joy, now that his passionate love (*érōs*, 540) and *póthos* (545) for his native land are satisfied. His opening speech is full of joyous light-symbolism, the gleam (*phéngos*) of day (504), the light (*pháos*) of the sun (508), the 'sun-facing' statues of the gods with brightness in their eyes (519–20), the glory of a victory 'that brings light in the night-time' (522). But a shadow falls when the Coryphaios talks of 'groaning from a darkened *phrēn*. This the Herald understands – presumably from the Coryphaios' tone of voice – to imply some feeling of abhorrence or loathing (*stúgos*, 547). Questioned on this, the Coryphaios adopts the precaution prescribed by the Watchman – 'silence as a remedy against harm'. Asked then, 'How so? Were you afraid of someone in the absence of the rulers?', he replies 'Yes, to the extent that death would have been a boon.' Once again fear has quenched joy.

The Herald returns to the theme of victory and success. He voices some self-pity and some *philanthrōpía* for the sufferings of the troops at Troy (with a touch of *stúgos* in 558ff.). But today, he concludes, is a day of brightness, a day for boasting and exultation, a time to dedicate bright spoils of armour in the temples of the gods.

587–614 Clytemnestra enters on a note of joy – joy at having been proved right about the meaning of the beacons despite the ridicule of male chauvinists like the chorus. Then she turns to a tricky task. She has to send a message to her husband that will both reassure him and also prevent the listening chorus from bursting out with a denial of what she says. She succeeds in this by skilful use of phrases that can be taken in two ways, as the Coryphaios hints in 615–16 (*allēgoría*).

One feature of the Queen's speech deserves special attention. In 605 she uses a distinctly erotic term (see F) to describe her husband, 'the darling (*erásmion*) of the city'. This word, as F notices, does not recur in Attic Greek until Plato. F describes it as 'undignified and almost offensive'. But it is a word that a loving wife might use with reference to her husband. Here, however, by adding 'of the city', she makes it clear 'to those who understand' that he certainly isn't *her* darling. Immediately afterwards, as if she feels that she has implied too much she goes on to assert that she 'destroyed no seal in the length of time and knew no delight nor blameful word from another man, any more than dyeings (or dippings) of bronze' (609–12). The surface meaning of the first phrase is obvious: husbands regularly sealed up their treasuries and storehouses when going abroad, as F amply documents. But the Triclinian Ms. has the interlinear gloss 'the seal of the conjugal bed'. F dismisses this as an 'absurd explanation', but HT and DP (quoting Herodas

1, 55) accept it, without amplification. Nor does F say why he thinks it absurd.

In fact the scholiast has good reason for his view. Aeschylus and everyone in his audience who was familiar with the *Odyssey* knew that Aigisthos had seduced Clytemnestra during Agamemnon's absence and had persuaded her to join in his plot to kill the King: see *Odyssey* 3, 263–6, 11, 421–3, and 24, 96–7. (Nothing is said about the murder of Iphigeneia in either epic: on the contrary if she is the Iphianassa named in *Iliad* 9, 145, she was still alive in the ninth year of the war.) Consequently the Queen's adultery would be in the minds of the poet and his audience. Also, no doubt, in the play itself, the citizens of Argos would also be expected to know about it. (Pindar in *Pythians* 11, 22–30, speculating on whether it was *érōs* for Aigisthos or revenge for Iphigeneia that motivated Clytemnestra mentions the gossip of citizens in such a case, and cf. 445ff. above.) On the other hand the citizens are unlikely to have had any certain knowledge of the plot to murder the King, though they might guess at it since Aigisthos had every reason to seek revenge. So the dark secret that the Watchman hinted at, and the *stúgos* mentioned in 547, are more likely to refer to the adulterous union than the intended murder.

The erotic implication of 'the seal' is strengthened by Clytemnestra's following denial of 'delight . . . from another man', as DP notices. Aeschylus in planning the play apparently chose to emphasize the revenge motive for Clytemnestra's crime, but at the same time he sustains what G. M. Hopkins called 'underthought' (cf. B. H. Fowler in *Dioniso* 49 (1978) 15–51, and *Eranos* 79 (1981) 1–22) about the sexual motive presented by Homer, until it becomes explicit in 1435ff. In *Frogs* 1043–4 Aristophanes makes Aeschylus say that, unlike Euripides, he never portrayed a lovesick woman in his plays. This is true so far as we know. But he undoubtedly presents the disastrous effects of *érōs* in the case of Helen and Cassandra. See further on 1224 and 1434ff.

The meaning of 'dyeings (or dippings) of bronze' in 612 is a notorious crux. Whatever it means, the chorus is likely to have felt a *frisson* of fear from its *allēgoría*, a fear doubtless enhanced by the sheer audacity of the whole speech and by the challenging demeanour of the Queen which would amount to saying 'I dare you to deny it.' Their reply contains an implicit warning for the Herald.

617–80 After Clytemnestra has gone back into the Palace the emotional tension relaxes again, and our thoughts and feelings are directed away from Argos for a while. There are mild contrasts of gladness and gloom in the Herald's account of what happened (636–7 and 667–9), with two references to divine anger (*kótos* in the question of the Coryphaios in 635, *mênis* in the reply, 649). The abnormal alliance of fire and water (650–1), and the personification of the storm as 'an evil shepherd' (657), and the description of the sea as being 'a-flower with corpses' (a truly Baudelairean phrase if *anthein* has full force in 659), are all images of *perverted nature*. Light-imagery recurs three times (658, 668, 676) and darkness once (653). The Herald's hope that the royal houses (of Agamemnon and Menelaos) will be saved from utter destruction by Zeus implies some latent fear.

681–749 The chorus are perturbed by the news of Menelaos' disappearance and by the Herald's sombre reference to 'the destruction of the race'. All this trouble, they assert, is the fault of a woman, Helen, who (as her name implies) brought Hell to ships and men and cities, and both kin and care (*kêdos* 699, see on *nomen omen*) to Troy. In their description of her light-hearted departure from Sparta the mood of voluptuous sensuality is strong, as we learn how she came out from the luxuriously woven curtains of her bedroom (or bed) and sailed away to Troy on the breeze of Zephyros (who according to one account was the father of Eros). The amorous ambiance is supported by the rhythm that breaks at 691–5 into *anacreontics*, the metre named after the poet of love and pleasure who lived in Athens when Aeschylus was a boy.

The romantic mood changes very quickly when 'many-manned hunters' (the epithet used of Helen in a very different sense in 62) follow on her track. Strife, Eris, takes over from Eros in 698 – Strife who, as the audience would remember, initiated the chain of events that led to the Trojan war when she hurled the golden apple inscribed 'For the fairest' among the goddesses on Olympus.

In 706–16 we have a brief movement from festive joy to grief and lamentation. The much discussed parable of the lion cub emblemizes a similar development from *cháris* and *philía* to savagery and destruction, as this charming welcome guest (like Paris and Helen at first) becomes an avenging sacrificer – 'and the house was bespattered with blood'. There is a brief lull in 739–49 (aptly expressed in iambics after trochees as Ll-J notes). In the description of Helen as that 'heart-stinging flower of *érōs* with a tender weapon (*oxymoron*) in her eyes' perhaps Aeschylus wishes us to remember 'the pitiful weapon' of the eyes of Iphigeneia in 241–2. DP argues that the lion cub is not simply a symbol of Helen but of all the circumstances leading to the sack of Troy (cf. Ll–J). In fact it probably symbolizes both ideas under the general notion of love and loveliness turning to savagery and destruction. A further variation on the theme of light-and-darkness is added in the complex antithesis between a house dark with smoke but bright with Justice and a palace bright with gold but dark with crime, a piece of *chiaroscuro* worthy of Rembrandt.

257–781 Recapitulation. We have been through many alternations of emotions in this part of the play – joy at the victory, anxiety at Clytemnestra's veiled threats and challenges, pity for the sufferings of both the Greeks and the Trojans, compassion for the *póthos* of Menelaos and for the grief of those who mourn dead kinsmen at Troy (and possibly sympathy for their anti-war resentment), scorn, perhaps, for the chorus's stupid anti-feminism, anxiety again when the Herald and chorus talk of dispirited gloom and a death-wish, a touch of *stúgos* at Clytemnestra's defiant lies, remote sympathy for the sufferings of the Greeks in the storm described by the Herald, and a bitter-sweet response to the glowing picture of that lethal and beautiful *femme fatale*, Helen. In the last three stanzas the prevailing mood is apprehension about what may happen to people at the height of their prosperity, such as (it is implied) victorious Agamemnon. Cf. 338–47.

782–809 The chorus anxiously do their best to warn Agamemnon against treachery and hypocrisy, but fail.

810–913 In this crucial confrontation between the King (with his concubine Cassandra) and the Queen, considerations of characterisation and plot are dominant. But one question of *êthos* must be answered before the degree of our pity, fear, hate and repulsion, towards both characters can be determined. Attitudes towards Agamemnon vary between F's whole-hearted admiration and DP's sharp fault-finding. Three points need to be kept in mind. First, the Watchman and the chorus plainly like him. Secondly, in his words to the chorus and the Queen he shows, as I see it, insensitivity and arrogance and – worse still to the Greek mind – stupidity. (Editors have missed a hint here: when he praises Odysseus as his only faithful and trustworthy friend at Troy the Athenian audience may well have thought 'Poor deluded man, to trust such a notorious deceiver.' The remark is meant, I believe, to show that Agamemnon just doesn't understand 'the mirror of society', as he claims in 839. His subsequent deception by his wife, despite the chorus's warnings, will prove this only too clearly.) Thirdly, to my mind there is a distinct touch of gloating, *epichairekakía*, in his description of the fate of Troy, especially in his remark about the 'fatty breaths of wealth' – note the expressive *p*-alliteration in the Greek – that rise from the burning city. (Older Athenians would remember the burning of Athens by the Persians twenty-two years earlier.) The same *Schadenfreude* is implied when he boasts that 'the fierce beast of Argos . . . the ravening lion licked his fill of princely blood' (827–8). The contrast between that kind of language and

Clytemnestra's sympathetic descriptions of the sorrows of the Trojans (320ff.) is not in his favour. (Incidentally the only time that Agamemnon mentions Clytemnestra in the *Iliad* is when he says he prefers his concubine Chryseis to her, in Book 1, 113.) In fact apart from the problematical degree of his moral culpability in sacrificing Iphigeneia he satisfies Aristotle's prescription for the best kind of tragic hero – a reasonably decent man with fatal flaws of judgment and character, though we may well feel that his punishment was excessive. If Agamemnon were such a model of kingly rectitude as F believes, his death would have been foul and repulsive (*miarós*) in Aristotle's view (*Poetics* 1452b 36).

As to Clytemnestra, we have seen and heard enough of her to know how formidable and yet how warmly imaginative she is. In *Odyssey* 3, 265–72, Nestor says that 'she was endowed with goodness of heart-and-mind (*phresí*)' until Aigisthos 'led her, in mutual willingness, to his home'. Aeschylus, I think, intends to give an impression of perverted goodness rather than of innate villainy.

Agamemnon's opening speech is coldly unemotional apart from the touches of *Schadenfreude* already noticed, and has a passing, but significant reference to *phthónos* in 833. In contrast, Clytemnestra's reply palpitates with warm, but hypocritical emotion and with extraordinarily rich imagery. She addresses the chorus first with a kind of warning challenge – 'I shall not be ashamed to tell my husband-loving (or 'man-loving') ways to you' (856–7) – 'And', the implication is, 'I dare you to deny them.' By using the ambiguous term *philánoras* (see on *anér*) she implies to the chorus (who used the same term in connection with Helen in 411) 'You know that this means Aigisthos to me, but Agamemnon doesn't.' F rejects the possibility of an intended double meaning here and warns readers against 'any concession to the playful ingenuity shown by Headlam, among others'. But gibes are not arguments, and readers less prejudiced against the notion that Aeschylus would not wish to remind his audience of Clytemnestra's notorious adultery may prefer the views of Headlam on this.

HT also finds erotic innuendoes – and rightly I believe – in two other phrases used by Clytemnestra in this speech. The first is 'bewailing the lamp-holdings even untended' (891). The primary reference is probably to the beacons (see F). But as HT fully establishes, the lamp is frequently mentioned in Greek poetry as a companion of erotic scenes (and cf. Artemidoros 67, 14–15). Secondly, as HT also notices, 'the time that slept with me' (894) suggests a very different kind of bedfellow. As I see it, such *allēgoríai* are Aeschylus' method of keeping the audience aware of the *stúgos* inside the palace, until it is blatantly revealed by Clytemnestra in 1431ff. At the end of her speech, as she orders the servants to spread the blood-coloured tapestries for Agamemnon to tread on, she uses another kind of *double entendre*, 'that Justice may bring him to an *unexpected* house-and-home', cf. Agamemnon's bitter remark about how he had hoped to be treated on his return home in *Odyssey* 11, 430–2.

When Agamemnon, wary, as he is, of divine as well as human *phthónos*, demurs at such an act of wanton pride and self-glorification as trampling on precious fabrics, Clytemnestra with brilliant dialectic first quells his religious scruples and then overcomes his *aidós* towards popular reproach by the clever aphorism 'The man who incurs no envy (in the bad sense, *phthónos*) is not enviable' (in the good sense, *zêlos* as defined in chapter 3). Her final argument is a subtle feminine one, 'You'll prove your power (*krátos* again) by willingly yielding to me on this' – a pretty phrase from a woman whose masculine power we have known since the Watchman's description of her in 11.

931–57 The tense and crucial thirteen lines of stichomythia in 931–44, a verbal duel for life or death, must have given the Athenian audience the kind of excitement that Romans would feel when a gladiator wielding the sword and shield of a warrior fought a wily *retiarius* with his entangling net and trident. Our pity and fear for Agamemnon when he yields must be tempered with recognition of his insensitive weakness and his folly in thinking that he can escape *phthónos* by having his shoes removed before he tramples on the tapestries and by a prayer. And how can one defend a man (from himself) who admits that he feels a great deal of *aidós* in destroying costly tapestries by walking on them, and then goes and does it? Clytemnestra defiantly rejected shame in 856. Agamemnon claims to feel *aidós*, but acts as if he had none.

Finally Agamemnon, with characteristic coldness towards the feelings of others, orders Clytemnestra to bring 'this stranger here graciously (or 'kindly') into the house' adding pious platitudes about heaven's favour towards the gentle use of *krátos* and about the unpleasantness of being a slave. 'Besides', he adds, 'she has come with me as the army's choice gift, a flower chosen out of many things of value.' After this suggestion that valuable things should be handled with care he proceeds to trample on the precious tapestries. F finds pity in Agamemnon's introduction of Cassandra. Perhaps he is right, but I find his words frigid, insensitive, hypocritical (how gently did Agamemnon use his *krátos* at Troy?) and egotistic. And how does Princess Cassandra like being described as a slave (cf. Clytemnestra's bitter variation on the same theme in 1035–45 and 1065–8)? And how does Clytemnestra like being ordered to be kind to her husband's concubine? In fact the Queen totally ignores Agamemnon's command and leaves Cassandra standing outside the palace.

F seems to be uncharacteristically off-balance in his treatment of this scene, perhaps because of his determination to defend Agamemnon. He scornfully rejects the view that the King has 'any other feeling for his captive beyond that of pity for her fate', meaning, I take it, that no *érōs* is involved. But Clytemnestra had no illusions about that (see on 1434ff. and cf. *Trojan Women* 252–5 and *Hecuba* 829). Secondly, F takes the view that Cassandra is not recognizable in this scene. Apart from Wilamowitz's suggestion that Cassandra's prophetic costume (cf. 1264–5) would make it clear that she was the famous prophetic princess of Troy, would anyone but the grossest ignoramus in the audience have failed to guess on the basis of the epic tradition, who this female companion of the King was? Aeschylus keeps her very much in the background so as not to distract attention from the main action. But her silent presence adds strongly to the emotional tension of this and the following scene.

The symbolism of the King's last words (apart from his death-cry) 'I go into the halls of the house trampling on crimson' and of his corresponding action has been fully explored elsewhere (see Goheen and Lebeck). But it is strange, in view of recent studies on the colours and colour-sense of the Greeks, that *porphúras* is still sometimes translated 'purple' here. The meanings of the word seem to have extended from brown to crimson, and here, of course, the colour will be that of blood.

958–74 The suspense becomes almost unbearable while Agamemnon moves towards the House of Death. It is shared by the chorus (who are anxious) and by Clytemnestra (who is hopeful) about the King's fate – and we in the audience must wonder, too, whether perhaps he will draw back, even though we know from the tradition that he is doomed to die. (If the acting and the language are compelling enough an audience may forget its foreknowledge and live by empathy in the present moment of the play.)

Clytemnestra's speech during Agamemnon's progress has been much criticized. DP, for example, finds 'an unsatisfactory muddle' in 961, while 965 is 'most abnormal' and the syntax of 966ff. is 'pitiable' and whatever the true reading may be there 'the sentence as a whole is inelegant enough'. DP also notes 'indifference to repetition' in the use of various words for 'house' in 961, 962, 964, 966, 968, 971, 972. But if we are to appreciate the dramatic and emotional power of the *finale* of this tremendous scene we should, perhaps, feel more pity for the persons concerned than for the syntax, and recognize that abnormal situations may provoke abnormal language. Here is a woman who has long been waiting and planning for this very climax. As Agamemnon advances towards the fatal door she fears that at any moment he may sense danger and withdraw (like Cassandra in 1306–11 and 1323), or else the chorus may dare to shout 'Don't go in' (cf. 1331–4).

As to the remarkable *repetitions* of references to the House of Death, if we accept the suggestion mentioned on 35–7 that the house, whose facade forms the permanent background to the whole play, has the force of a silent character throughout (on this see especially Jones 82–111), then we may take it that Aeschylus here intends to intensify our awareness of its sinister menace. A modern stage-manager would effect this by projecting a lurid spotlight on it. Deprived of such mechanical aids Aeschylus has to use words, though he has also already employed one simple but ingenious visual aid, the red fabrics that point to the fatal door. This is the first scene in which the house plays an obtrusive part as a thing to promote terror. But Aeschylus has been consistently leading up to this by no less than twenty-six previous references to the house – first the five already noticed in the Watchman's speech, and then twenty-one spaced over the intervening scenes (155, 157, 208, 244, 310, 343, 409, 415, 427, 518, 579, 606, 679, 851, 862, 865, 867, 897, 911, 914, 948). This frequency can be partly explained by the fact that the genre of this play is a home-coming, a macabre *nóstos*. But it is partly, I believe, a means of highlighting the abominable house with its pitiful and fearful deeds in the past, present, and future. The house will again be thrown into ghastly prominence in 1306ff. (Eugene O'Neill makes a similarly effective use of the Mannion's home in his modern version of the *Oresteia, Mourning Becomes Electra*, and cf. Poe's 'Fall of the House of Usher'.)

The primary function of this extraordinary speech of Clytemnestra is to hold the attention of Agamemnon by talking, talking, talking, for fear that a moment of silence would let him change his mind. Some of the effusive symbolism has sinister undertones. 'Ever-renewed ooze of crimson . . . for the dyeing of garments' recalls the saffron-dyed robes of Iphigeneia and 'the dyeing of bronze' (cf. on 239). The word for 'of garments' here (*heimátōn*), repeated in 963, is

phonetically close to *haimátōn*, meaning 'of blood-flows'. HT
suggests that 'wine from the unripe grape' (970) refers to the
shedding of Iphigeneia's blood, since *ómphax* is used elsewhere to mean 'a young virgin'. F dismisses this as 'an un-
warranted psychological nicety'. But what is more likely to
be in the Queen's mind here than the first reason for her
revenge? In general the basic pattern of the imagery here –
root-leaf-grape, coolness-heat-cold, summer-winter-autumn
– resembles the free associations of a patient undergoing
psychological analysis. It is true that the total effect is incoherent. But such language and thought is apt for moments of
high emotional tension. Bernard Shaw in the *Saturday Review*
for 20 March 1897 observed on Cleopatra's outburst at the
death of Antony in *Antony and Cleopatra*, beginning

> Oh withered is the garland of the war,
> The soldier's pole is fallen. . . .

'This is not good sense – not even good grammar. If you ask
what does it all mean, the reply must be that it means just what
its utterer feels. The chaos of its thought is a reflection of her
mind. . . .'

975–1034 Here we have the most effective expression of
taraché and of anxious, ill-defined fear in Greek tragedy.
Visual imagery – dread is seen as 'fluttering' like a distressed
bird in front of their hearts – merges into aural imagery – an
unwanted, boding song – and merges back again into the visual
image of baffling dreams. Then the chorus sing of the cause of
their mental and emotional distress: their *phrēn* should be
confident and hopeful now that victory has been won and the
King is home again, but their *thumós* 'from inside' keeps
chanting 'a dirge of the Erinyes'. The use of *thumós*, 'passion',
here (as in the very similar *Persians* 10–11) is noteworthy. As
noticed in chapter 3, it is the irrational hard-to-control,
dynamic element in the *psuché*. The chorus find it irrepressible
here. In fact, they go on to sing, one must believe what one's
entrails (*splánchna*) 'sing' at a time like this, and one must heed

what is predicted by 'the heart as it whirls in eddies that bring fulfilment against the justified mind' – a strange maelstrom of meaning indeed! But such language is what one would expect in cases of extreme *taraché*. The dominant image of a whirling vortex symbolizes this mental and emotional condition more powerfully than the commoner image of a *storm* at sea. The rhythms of these two stanzas, short, catalectic trochaic dimeters – broken by a swift run of dactyls in the fifth lines – has been compared to the beat of a palpitating heart. The dactyls have another significance: they are apt for prophetic utterances (cf. on 104ff.).

In the desperately corrupt third stanza the mind gains control of the 'entrails' for a while in some pious philosophizing. But in the fourth stanza the thought of 'a man's blood falling to the earth in death' soon sets their *taraché* fluttering again in another highly controversial passage which I paraphrase as: 'It was Moira (whose function is to see that everything keeps to its own appointed sphere) who prevented Asklepios from successfully trespassing on Death's territory by restoring a man to life (1022–4): the same goddess prevents my heart from usurping the province of my tongue by telling me in plain words what it is trying to say. Consequently my heart can only murmur in darkness, with agonizing *thumós*, and without any hope of spinning off a timely thread (of rational discourse), while my *phrēn* is all ablaze.' The 'timely thread' means some intelligible word-and-thought (*lógos*) spun from the turbulent heart in the same way as a continuous thread is spun from a tangled mass of wool. (Aeschylus himself is accused of using 'concepts like tangled wool' in 'Longinus' 15, 5, and of talking 'like a holm-oak on fire' in *Frogs* 859.) The 'conflagration' of the heart-and-mind is a striking variation of the recurrent flame of fire motif, combining the notions of heart and force. In simplest terms the passage expresses a commonplace of poetry ancient and modern – the impossibility of expressing the deepest emotions in lucid words. Whether or not Aeschylus is on the verge of realizing the existence of the unconscious here I leave to psychologists to decide.

1035–71   Instead of letting Agamemnon's death-cry ring out at once, or else introducing an agitated messenger to announce his death, as we might have expected, Aeschylus stretches suspense here and in the following scene almost to the breaking point. The futile effort of the Queen to lure Cassandra into the palace – 'Will you walk into my parlour, said the Spider to the Fly?' – is ethical rather than emotional, though the Queen makes a passing reference to divine *mênis* in 1036 and then flares up angrily herself. Next, Aeschylus modulates from the key of fear and anger to the key of pity in the remark of the Coryphaios that Cassandra is like a newly caught animal (a comparison which Clytemnestra distorts into that of a senseless unbroken-in horse straining with bleeding mouth at the bit) to a direct statement, after the Queen has gone, 'I pity her and will not be angry.' Pity dominates now.

It is not clear why Aeschylus allowed Clytemnestra to be morally defeated by Cassandra in this brief interlude. The best explanation, perhaps, is that the scene gives stature to Cassandra and at the same time emphasizes her tense stillness just before her appalling shrieks in 1072ff. (D. C. C. Young in *CQ* 14 (1963) 15 finds a sexual *kakémphaton* in *tríbein* in 1056, but the context hardly suggests it there as it does in 1439ff.)

1072–1135   The germ of the heart-rending scene that follows was perhaps what the ghost of Agamemnon said in Hades in describing his own death (*Odyssey* 11, 421), 'I heard the most pitiful (*oiktrotátēn*) cry of Priam's daughter Cassandra, whom deceitful Clytemnestra killed beside me.' Aeschylus has expanded this into an amazingly effective episode – the second wave in his *trikumía* of pitiful deaths. At first Cassandra's agony of terror and grief can only be screamed out in repeated *exclamatory cries* and invocations of Apollo. Articulate speech then evolves by way of a *nomen omen* in which Apollo's name is seen to incorporate a verb meaning to destroy in Greek (like Apollyon in *The Pilgrim's Progress*). Her next object of conscious recognition is the House of Death, which she describes in terms reminiscent of the phrase in *Odyssey* 11, 420,

'The whole floor steamed with blood.' She is reacting at first to the abominable crime of Atreus in feasting Thyestes with his children's flesh. Clairvoyantly she can hear the babies bewailing their fate. Immediately afterwards she sees the imminent horror of the death of Agamemnon entangled in 'the net'. This is described in quick-flash, impressionistic 'shots' – the brightness of the victim's body after the bath, 'hand reaching out from hand' (like a fisherman's when he draws in a net), and, marked by screams of *é, é, papaî*, the 'net of Death'. The chorus represented by the Coryphaios, have been replying up to this in calm iambic trimeters to the irregular lyric metres (partly *dochmiac*) of Cassandra – in a matter-of-fact detached way like elderly uncles dealing with a hysterical niece. The change to dochmiacs in 1121 shows that they have begun to react physically to her fearful utterances. They feel their 'saffron' blood running back to their hearts as if they had been fatally wounded by a spear.

With two gasps of horror – the sharply accented *á á* seems the best reading here, in contrast with the *â* discussed in chapter 8 – Cassandra sees the murder of Agamemnon taking place. It is so real to her that she cries out for someone to stop it: 'Keep the bull from the cow.' The metaphor may have sexual undertones as in 245, but if so they are fainter here. The following phrase 'She has caught him with the black contrivance of the horned one' (F) or (preferably, I think) 'with the black-horned device' is obscure – a nightmarishly vague and terrifying image like 'that two-handed engine at the door' in Milton's *Lycidas*. The Coryphaios and chorus respond in an iambic trimeter followed by dochmiacs as in 1119–24 – an alternation of cool reasoning and excited emotionalism as before.

1136–77 Cassandra now changes from horrified clairvoyance about the King's death to self-pity and pity for her kinsfolk. The chorus, now completely emotional, as the metre shows, compare her – conventionally – to that traditional emblem of sad, but melodious lamentation, the nightingale, who with piteous *phrénes* bewails Itys her son, eaten, like Thyestes' children, by his father. Pathetically Cassandra rejects the comparison as inept (the analytical Greek mind operates even at a moment of high emotion), since the nightingale lives on in a life of sweet melody while she is doomed to 'cleaving asunder by the two-edged weapon'. (Her voice as she prophesies this has 'an ill-boding clang', like that of Calchas in 156 and 201.) In 1156ff. her self-pity turns to pitiful lamentation for the fate of Priam and Troy. The chorus find her prediction of her own death 'shattering to hear', and feel helplessly uncertain about the outcome.

Meanwhile, as the rhythm slows, Cassandra has been gradually growing calmer in iambic trimeters in 1148–9, 1160–1, and 1171–2, while the chorus grow more excited.

1178ff. Now, in regular iambic trimeters, Cassandra discards emotional rhythms and images and turns to rational statement for a while. But a new feeling is expressed in 1192, *stúgos*, disgust – expressed by *spitting* – for the crimes of Atreus and Thyestes. (Artemis felt the same way about 'the feast of the eagles' in 137.) This prepares the way for the third, and most emphatic expression of loathing in 1228ff. Next *érōs* reappears, here in the form of the vengeful passion of Apollo. The pangs of prophecy seize Cassandra again in 1214, as her screams indicate, whirling her (cf. 907) in *taraché* for a moment before she sees the ghastliest vision of all, the children of Thyestes surrealistically holding the intestines and entrails that their own father ate, 'a pitiful burden to bear'. The first overt reference to Aigisthos in the play follows immediately. He, as a Pelopid, is entitled to the family emblem of the lion, but the symbol is perverted by an *oxymoron* in Cassandra's phrase 'a weakling lion'. (Cf. Shakespeare, *Troilus and Cressida* 3, 2: 'They that have the voice of lions and the act of hares, are they not monsters?') She adds a frankly sexual description of him as 'wallowing in the bed', and then (1228) she turns to describe the Queen as a 'lewd hound' (*misétēs*: see F on the accentuation). Then Cassandra evokes a menagerie of evil and hateful animals and monsters (as discussed in chapter 8) to express how she loathes her.

The Coryphaios says that he shuddered and felt fear at the description of the fate of the children of Thyestes but is at a loss about the reference to future events (Aeschylus presumably intends the obtuseness of these Argive Elders to increase our sympathy for Cassandra.) So she bluntly tells them that Agamemnon is doomed. The Coryphaios repudiates this notion and adds a conventional gibe about the obscurity of oracles. This incredulity reminds Cassandra of the curse of Apollo and she breaks into screams of agony again. She goes on to repeat her prediction of her own death at the hand of 'the two-footed lioness lying with the wolf in the absence of the truly noble lion' (again the sexual reference in this monstrous mating of different beasts). In anger at the gift of prophecy that betrayed her she throws off the symbols of her prophetic vocation, denounces Apollo, predicts the revenge that Orestes will exact, and turns to address the door of the House as 'gates of Hades', adding a prayer that at least the stroke that kills her may be immediately mortal. (Compare the similarly cautious prayer of the chorus in 1448–51.)

Here (1295–6) the Coryphaios pityingly addresses the Prophetess as 'a woman of much misfortune and of much wisdom as well', but adds 'that was a long speech' (like Agamemnon to Clytemnestra in 916) – more of the blatant male chauvinism in this play (but F doesn't think so). A brief, tense argument in stichomythia is broken up when Cassandra shrinks back as she approaches the door. The Coryphaios thinks she is frightened, but it is more disgust than fear as shown by her exclamations, *pheû*, *pheû* and by the Coryphaios' subsequent word *stúgos*. What has disgusted her, she explains, is 'the reek from the house as from a tomb'.

Courageously, however, Cassandra goes forward towards the evil door, with what sounds like her last words – 'Enough of life' (1314). Then Aeschylus produces a masterstroke of *éleos*. Momentarily her courage fails her. For the first time she begins an appeal for help – she is only a young woman now,

151

another Iphigeneia, not a god-possessed prophetess. She calls to the chorus 'Oh, oh, *xénoi* . . .' and then breaks off in *aposiopesis*. The meaning of that untranslatable word *xénos* here (already used unemphatically by Cassandra in 1299) is certainly not just 'strangers' which in English primarily suggests alienation. On the contrary the word appeals to that basic rule of Greek ethics, *philoxenía* the duty of kindness to 'the stranger within the gates'. Her appeal, then, is almost as strong as a Christian's appeal 'For Christ's sake'. But she stops herself – 'No indeed (*oútoi*: many editors ignore the force of the emphatic particle), I am not going to raise a frightened cry like a bird at a bush where danger lurks'. . . . (See F for other interpretations.)

After this stifled appeal for help Cassandra steels her heart by thinking of revenge. The Coryphaios, ignoring her formal request to the chorus to act as witnesses when the day of retributive justice comes, offers his last tribute of compassion – 'O woman of much suffering, I pity you for your god-predicted fate!' Cassandra reiterates her desire for revenge. There she might have said her last words. But with a further masterly touch Aeschylus makes her rise above her personal feelings in last words whose tone contrasts sharply with the passionate shrieks, denunciations, and imprecations, of her earlier utterances:

> Alas for mortal doings. When they're prosperous
> One may compare them to a shadow. If they fare ill,
> A touch of a wet sponge wipes their picture out –
> And this I pity more than the other fate.

It is supremely moving that in her last moment Cassandra transcends all self-regarding feelings in compassionate *philanthrōpía* and *Weltschmerz*. F comments: 'The resigned wisdom of Cassandra's last words is perhaps more deeply moving than all her ecstacies', but this is to over-emphasize the intellectual aspect. What Aeschylus emphasizes is not her wisdom, but the fact that she shows such pity for others when she is in such pitiable misfortune herself.

1331–42 When Cassandra has gone into the House of Death – with her head high, one may guess, as befits a princess – the chorus, taking up her remark about prosperity and disaster, link it with a symbolical house of disastrous prosperity where no one warns 'Don't enter.' (Here Aeschylus' usual symbolical progression is reversed: the actual entry into a house comes before the metaphorical event – and perhaps the phrase 'Don't enter' reflects what the chorus feel they should have said to both Agamemnon and Cassandra.) Then, though still not quite convinced about the King's death, they moralize briefly about its 'lesson'. The metre, regular anapaests, reflects their rather surprisingly unexcited mood. Perhaps they march around slowly and meditatively to its rhythm. Presumably Aeschylus is aiming at a moment of *calm* before the storm breaks.

1343–71 The King's two terrible death-cries ring out. They are the first death-cries in extant Greek tragedy (see Taplin, 1976, 103), and the most resonant of all. We who encounter them first in cold print must make a great effort of imagination to realize what they would have sounded like when uttered with all the emotional power of a dedicated actor's voice in the Theatre of Dionysos. When they come from inside the dark door, it is almost as if, in the Watchman's words, the House had been given a voice. The chorus is slow to react emotionally, though the introduction for a moment of catalectic trochaic tetrameters (1344, 1346–7) indicates their perturbation. Cautious old men that they are, they deliberate on what should be done, some diffidently, others boldly, others uncertainly. There is not a single expression of emotion in the whole debate. The *ékplēxis* of the King's cries has numbed their feelings but not their minds though some degree of *taraché* prevails (cf. 1358–61).

1372–98 Into this state of perplexity Clytemnestra's defiant appearance standing over the corpses of her victims comes like a blaze of lurid light through darkness. No indecision, no uncertainty, here, only terse realism. The image of the net is now actualized in her gloating description of how she entangled the King in 'an evil wealth of dress' (*oxymoron*). She says all of this in the present tense and presumably with expressive gestures. But the most atrocious part (*stúgos*) of her speech comes when she says, 'As he belches forth his life where he lay, spurting out a thin jet of blood, he strikes me with a dark shower of gory dew, and I rejoice no less than the sown fields rejoice at the god-given brightness (of the dew) when the birth-pangs of the ear are at hand.' Here is *perverted nature imagery* at its height. The pure life-giving dew from heaven has become blood pouring from a murdered husband: the joy of the cornfields when their grain comes to the birth has become the fiendish *epichairekakía* of a vengeful wife. Emblems of fruitfulness are turned into symptoms of death.

If the word translated 'belches' above (*orugánei*, Hermann's emendation accepted by F, HT, and R, but not by DP or G) is authentic, it is a *hapax* in Greek tragedy. As F remarks 'the coarseness of expression fits in with Clytemnestra's ferocity' (see on 1435ff. below). But the emendation is far from being certain.

1399–1430 The Coryphaios, speaking in unemotional iambic trimeters, expresses at first only astonishment (which is a mild form of *ékplēxis*) at the Queen's brutal and defiant words. When she replies with unmitigated boldness, the whole chorus react more emotionally, mainly in *dochmiacs*. They threaten her with punishment and the hatred of the people (*némesis*). Metrically from 1407–61 we have the reverse of the Cassandra scene, the chorus chanting in lyric metres, the Queen replying calmly in iambic trimeters. She defends herself as in a court of law – Agamemnon murdered her daughter; is she not justified in her retaliation? The chorus reply that she must be mad, and she must die.

1431–47 Clytemnestra, weakening a little in her self-reliance, asserts, 'Expectancy (*elpís*) does not tread for me in the hall of Fear while Aigisthos kindles fire on my hearth (*hestía*) remaining loyal to me.' The metaphor is generally taken as meaning 'while Aigisthos continues to be the legitimate lord of the house' with reference to family sacrifices at the hearth-stone. That may be so. But 'lighting the fire' is not the same as performing a sacrifice, so, in view of the undeniable sexual implications of the succeeding lines, a different meaning may be intended here. (As we have seen, Cassandra has already spoken, in 1224, of Aigisthos as 'wallowing in the bed', and she has called the Queen 'lewd' in 1228.) The two words for 'hearth' in Greek, *hestía* and *eschára*, definitely had sexual meanings (see Aristophanes, *Knights* 1286; Epicrates 10; Eustathius, 815, 13; 1539,33; Henderson 130–48). Arte-midoros (Hercher 98, 9–12) states that to dream of someone kindling fire on a *hestía* means the begetting of children 'for at that time a woman grows hotter'. On the other hand *hestía* in 427, 968, and 1056, is less likely to have any such overtones since the context does not suggest eroticism. Here it is the mention of Aigisthos that suggests sexual implications in the Queen's imagery.

Clytemnestra's language becomes overtly erotic in 1439ff. as F admits. She describes Agamemnon as 'the soothing thing (*meíligma*, used in *Odyssey* 10, 217 of bits thrown to dogs) of the Chryseids (contemptuous plural) at Troy'. Then, with no justification – Cassandra had no choice, poor girl – she lashes out at Cassandra's reputation calling her, in a unique phrase 'mast-rubber' (*histotríbēs*: attempts to emend this word are convincingly rejected by F, DP and R).

Several editors (see F) have assumed a sexual *kakémphaton* here, but they have generally, like F, held that the less said about that the better: Ll-J, DP, and R, find the reference to a mast unintelligible. But the fact is that the terms 'mast' and 'rubbing' have clear and obvious erotic implications elsewhere in Greek literature (see G. L. Koniaris, W. B. Tyrrell, and E. K. Borthwick, in *AJP* 101–2 (1980, 1981), 42–4, 44–6, and 1–2: also Henderson 49, 161–4, 176 and Young as cited on 1056: to their references add the testimony of the Archbishop of Thessalonica, Eustathius 1760, 24–7).

As I see it, then, Aeschylus has deliberately used an obscene term to express the strength of Clytemnestra's other motive for killing the King, namely, sexual hate resulting from his adultery with Chryseis and Cassandra (who asserts the same motive in 1263). Even though the Queen is an adulteress herself now – Homer implies in *Odyssey* 3, 265–6 that her seduction by Aigisthos took time – she is infuriated by the fact that Agamemnon has shamed her by bringing Cassandra home as a concubine. (Cf. Hermione's jealousy of Andromache in *Andromache*.) The dramatic function of the term, like that of *ataúrotos* in 244 is presumably to cause a mild *ékplēxis*, as well as to accentuate our *stúgos* for Clytemnestra and our pity for Cassandra.

The sexual imagery continues in 1446–7, though here, too, many editors are reluctant to admit it – 'There she lies, his lover, and she has brought me a relish (or side-dish, an extra titbit, *paropsónēma*) of my bed (*eunês*), of my luxury (*khlidês*).' F rejects *eunês* as corrupt on the grounds that 'it is difficult to imagine Clytemnestra speaking of the joys of her bed in a tone such as Hamlet uses to his mother' (why?) and because Clytemnestra's *khlidé* is confined to what she says in 1391–2 (again why?). He adds 'the lust which wholly possesses the soul of this daemonic woman at the great climax of her life is not sexual, but lust for revenge'. This assertion ignores what Homer said about the Queen (cf. on 503–86), and what Pindar says about 'the nightly couchings that led her astray when she was being tamed in a different bed' (*Pythians* 11, 24–5), and what Euripides makes her say in *Electra* 1030ff. where she alleges that the bringing home of Cassandra, not the killing of Iphigeneia, caused her to kill her husband.

HT, HP, G, Ll-J, and R, accept a sexual implication in *paropsónēma* and cite parallels, though not from tragedy (cf. Henderson 144). If this view is correct the Queen's gibe shows a mixture of hate, jealousy and *epichairekakía* which, as soon appears, arouses sheer revulsion in the chorus and in the audience.

On the other hand the passing reference to Cassandra's

'swan song' (1444–5) is hardly in keeping with the mocking tone of the rest of the speech. It sounds like the voice of the poet himself introducing what F calls 'a soft and moving echo' of Cassandra's voice in the previous scene. T. S. Eliot in *Poetry and Drama* discusses a similar emergence of the poet's voice in *Hamlet* when Horatio says

> So have I heard and do in part believe . . .
> But, look, the morn, in russet mantle clad,
> Walks o'er the dew of yon high eastern hill
> Break we our watch up. . . .

Eliot suggests that here is 'a kind of musical design which reinforces and is one with the dramatic movement' and which 'has checked and accelerated the pulse of our emotion without knowing it' . . ., and so 'we are lifted for a moment beyond character'. The effect is, I think, similar on Clytemnestra's lips. The swan image is part of the last reference to Cassandra in the play, and the poet may feel that he cannot let it be entirely at the mercy of her bitter and malevolent murderer.

1448–61 Filled with disgust that their Queen should use such language and reveal such ugly feelings, the chorus (with the same exclamation of loathing, *pheû*, that Cassandra used in 1307) wish for death and then with typical anti-feminist prejudices they find it particularly distressing that their 'kindest protector' should have died at a woman's hand. They go on to sing of Helen's madness, an *érōs* that turned to *éris* (cf. 698).

1462–1512 *Significant rhythm*: Clytemnestra now begins to argue with the chorus (until 1576) in anapaests (which the chorus began to use in 1455). Presumably this congruence of rhythms indicates that she is beginning to feel sympathy for the despair and grief of the Argive elders, while, in turn, their emotions are becoming less violent. The Queen's words correspond to the implications of this change of rhythm. She is no longer brutally vindictive. She deprecates the chorus's death-wish and defends Helen from their rancour (*kótos*). In reply the chorus turn their minds away from her and – almost like Cassandra – visualize the daemon of the accused House, 'settling like a hateful raven' on the body of the King. (As already noted, to dream of a raven, according to Artemidoros indicates an adulterer.) Clytemnestra seizes on this line of defence – 'That's right: the thrice-glutted daemon of the race is to blame.' The chorus agree, 'Yes, it is the embodiment of wrath *mênis*.' Then they give expression to the wave of compassionate grief that sweeps over them at last, by singing the moving refrain that has been analysed in chapter 7. It contains a potent symbol of revulsion and fear towards Clytemnestra in the phrase, 'There you lie in this web of a spider.' If Aeschylus and his audience knew that some female spiders kill their mates (cf. Devereux 333) the symbol is specially relevant here, but there is no evidence for that knowledge. (On the other hand if the meaning is simply 'this woven spider-web', as F takes it, then the symbolism lapses, but that is weaker and less Aeschylean to my mind.) Possibly the reference to the 'Spider Mountain' in 309 was a deliberate foreshadowing of this.

1497–1576 The chorus, being a male and not a female chorus, dwell more on the legalistic aspects of the Queen's crime than on their sorrow for the King, though the repetition of the refrain and the additional lamentation in 1538–50 sustain a note of sorrow. Clytemnestra replies mainly in legalistic terms. She shows a flash of her former imagination in her sarcastic description of how Iphigeneia will, no doubt, fittingly welcome Agamemnon's spirit in Hades with an embrace and a kiss. Her vigorous defence reduces the chorus again (cf. 1530–2) to helplessness (*amēchania* 1561).

1577–1611 Joy, the evil joy of getting a brutal revenge – which we are expected to dislike, not to share – returns for a moment with the entry of Aigisthos and his invocation of 'the kindly gleam of a day that has brought justice'. To justify his triumph he describes in ghastly detail the abominable feast given to his father Thyestes by Agamemnon's father Atreus.

One word in his description offers another example of Aeschylus' use of a brutal word to shock his hearers. Aigisthos says that when his father discovered that he was eating his own children's flesh he 'vomited'. The word used, *erôn*, does not occur elsewhere, nor do any of its cognates (see LSJ) in Greek tragedy. In other instances of *stúgos* the reaction is to spit, as in 1192. But here the reaction is literally more visceral, because the degree of revulsion is at the highest possible pitch. (The only other term in tragedy to equal the 'coarseness' of this expression, together with *ataúrōtos* in 244 and *histotríbēs* in 1443, is the Nurse's reference to the 'urine-letting' of the infant Orestes in *Libation-bearers* 756, but that is a matter of the Nurse's *êthos* rather than of any *páthos*.)

1612–73 The chorus react with *némesis* and contempt to Aigisthos's rodomontade. Ll-J notes (on 1624) that his constant use of trite sayings and comparisons (cf. 1617–20, 1628–32, 1641–2, 1668) helps to reveal the contemptible meanness of his character. Their scornful word for him, 'Woman!', reverses the motif of the mannish woman that began in 11. The notion of perversion is carried on, more ornamentally, in Aigisthos's reply: 'Your tongue is the opposite of Orpheus's: he by his voice led everything after him in joy, but you by your puerile yelpings provoke hostility.' As the interchanges of taunts and threats become more excited the iambic trimeters change to catalectic trochaic tetrameters (1649ff.)

Clytemnestra's attempt to make peace contains her strongest affirmation of affection in the play, when she says 'Dearest of men' to Aigisthos. Her metaphor from reaping a harvest has nothing perverse about it. She attempts a reconciliation by addressing the chorus as 'reverend elders', and by remarking, not ironically this time, I think, 'That's a woman's saying if anyone thinks fit to learn from it.' When she fails to stop the bickering, her impatience – as with Cassandra – flares up again, and with it her masterfulness: 'Don't heed their futile yelpings. You and I, sharing the *krátos* over the House will settle things well.' But, as the next play shows, the House and its curse are beyond their power to control.

The overall effect of this scene is to create a state of *tarachḗ* which, together with the references to Orestes, keeps the audience in suspense for the next play of this integrated trilogy, just as in serial 'thrillers' in the cinema each episode used to end at a moment of crisis. *Libation-bearers* concludes with a similar state of *taragmós* in Orestes' mind and heart (1056).

Looking back over the intense emotionalism of this play one may find clarification of its emotional vicissitudes in statistics (approximate because the references are not always definite). References to grief in general are by far the most frequent (about twenty-seven). Joy comes next with about twelve. Then come anger (nine), *philía* (eight), pity (seven), and *érōs* (six). Fear and hate have five appearances each, and next to them are anxiety, *stúgos*, *philanthrōpía*, *ékplēxis* (three each), *póthos*, *némesis*, *aidṓs*, *tarachḗ* and an unspecified passion (two each). I leave it to others, if they wish, to make a fuller investigation of these frequencies with adequate discussion of the less definite references. But the general picture given here is, I believe, correct in outline, and it shows what a wide range of emotions is used in this the *Appassionata* of Aeschylus.

Some of the references are quite unemphatic. Others are emphasized by personification or extended descriptions, as we have seen. But even the least emphatic references could have an emotional effect subconsciously. Psychologists have studied the effect of subliminal advertisement in films or on television, when commercial slogans are flashed on the screen so fast that the eye cannot consciously perceive them, but – as some believe – the unconscious receives the message. (See N. F. Dixon, *Subliminal Perception: the Nature of a Controversy*, London 1971.) In other words we can have, it is believed, perception without awareness. It may be, then, that the same principle holds in the audial sphere, so that even very brief references as, for example, those to *phthónos* in 134 and to *némesis* (again by implication) in 456–7 and 140–11, have a lasting effect.

The change to a female chorus in *Libation-bearers* enables Aeschylus to compensate for the rather brief lamentations of the Argive Elders in *Agamemnon* with a *kommós* that lasts for over a hundred and fifty lines (306–478). Besides grief, almost all the other main tragic emotions are given scope in this play –fear, anger, hate, disgust and joy. In the climactic scene when Clytemnestra bares her breast – the breast from which, as she pleads, Orestes had 'drowsily drawn the nourishing milk with his gums' (896–8) – in the hope of escaping death at his hands, it is Orestes' necessary rejection of natural *storgē* for his mother that is most pitiful. Here the motif of *perverted nature* is taken from the Queen and given to the Prince. The same transference takes place with the recurrent symbolical image of the *snake*. In 249, 994 and 1047 the snake is Clytemnestra, as in Cassandra's description of her as an *amphísbaina* in *Agamemnon* 1233. But in her dream as described in 526–34 (see Devereux 182–218) the snake that draws blood from her breast must be Orestes. A clear analogy between this woman who kills her mate and is killed in turn by her offspring is noticed by Aelian in his treatise on the characteristics of animals when he describes (1, 24) how the female viper (*échidna* as in 249, 994) similarly kills and is killed. (Knowledge of this characteristic of vipers goes back at least to Herodotos 3, 109: see further in Devereux 177–8 and Lebeck's index at 'serpent'.) Characteristically Aeschylus embodies these metaphorical serpents in the 'thick-set snakes' of the Erinyes in 1050. Finally, after the deaths of the Queen and Aigisthos the third wave – or storm as the chorus calls it in 1066 – has spent itself.

In the appearance of the Furies at the beginning of *Eumenides* all the earlier references to *stúgos* reach their climax, and all the metaphorical monsters are surpassed by these hideous, bloodthirsty, loathsome, fearsome, angry and ferocious creatures with their threats of atrocious diseases. In them, too, the sporadic metaphors from hunting in the earlier plays (see Lebeck's index at 'hounds') become part of the action and of the visual effects. Their conversion by Athene into 'the Kindly Ones' is hardly plausible in terms of the arguments used, but it would be fully acceptable emotionally to Athenians in the optimistic atmosphere of the 450s BC.

One emotional element in *Eumenides* is unique in Greek tragedy. This is the weird incantation, the 'Binding Song' that is chanted and danced by the Furies in 307–96. In it Aeschylus plays on primitive fears of black magic and witchcraft as Shakespeare does in *Macbeth* – and both poets were dealing with audiences that fully believed in such things. (The modern equivalent might be a chorus of nuclear missiles or of cancer tumours.) Its audial effects reinforcing the fearsome conceptual meanings, deserve closer study than they have received as yet.

But the masterstroke of Aeschylean symbolical synthesis (as discussed in chapter 8) comes at the end of the trilogy when the vacillating imagery of light and darkness is consummated in a great crescendo of joy in 996ff., while the blood-coloured and blood-stained fabrics and robes of the two previous plays are sublimated in the red cloaks of the metics (see 1018 and 1028, and cf. *Agamemnon* 57 and *Libation-bearers* 971). Similarly the 'nestlings', both human and avian who suffered in the earlier plays (e.g. *Agamemnon* 50f. and *Libation-bearers* 256) have become the happy citizens of Athens gathered under the protective wings of their patron goddess in 1001–2.

The supreme glory of this *finale* is in its triumphant celebration of joy and illumination. There had been a false dawn at the end of *Libation-bearers* when the chorus sang 'Now we can see the light' (961), but the darkness soon returned. Here at long last we have the true radiance of lasting thanksgiving and gladness. Six times the chorus and Athene cry 'Be joyful' (*chaírete*), and the last words of the final refrain bring us back to the primeval way of expressing joy – 'Cry aloud now at our songs-and-dances' (*molpaí*: see in chapter 4). We may well believe that all the Athenians in the audience shared these joyful cries and songs and dances in this magnificent affirmation of the civilizing power of their city. The effect is like that of the Hymn to Joy of Beethoven (and Schiller) at the end of his ninth and last symphony. But here the joy is expressed visually as well as audially, with *lumière* as well as *son*.

This is the happiest ending in all Greek tragedy, happiest for the characters in the play and happiest for the audience. It contains all the kinder emotions of tragedy – joy, *philanthrōpía*, love of one's native land, civic pride, and *elpís* in its good sense. It affirms that under the aegis of Athena – that is, under Athenian piety and democracy at their best – primitive blood-feuds and monstrous crime will be banished by the rule of justice. Athenians could gladly believe this in 458 BC. Sad that within a lifetime this belief was shattered when the Athenians forgot what Aeschylus had made the chorus sing in *Agamemnon* 381–4, 'There is no shelter for a man when once in surfeit of wealth he has kicked the great altar of Justice into obscurity.'

CHAPTER TEN

The ultimate effect?

The emphasis in the previous chapters on the emotional and sensory elements of Greek tragedy could give three wrong impressions. First, it might be taken to imply that the intellectual element is unimportant. Such an opinion would be too obviously absurd to need any detailed refutation. Clearly the long stretches of exposition, argument and debate in which the emotional and sensory elements are muted have great importance in the total effect of any drama. On the other hand the view prevalent among scholars that these rational passages are supremely important needs, I believe, reconsideration if the evidence presented in this book is valid. These cerebral passages always have emotional undertones derived from the imagery, rhythm and voice-melody. There is no 'pure reason' in tragedy.

The second possible wrong impression is the reverse of this. There is no pure emotion in tragedy either, except perhaps in those terrible exclamatory cries that were considered in chapter 4. In nature the emotions are not separable from the mind and from the senses. As a theoretical concept they are useful for analysis, but when it comes to dealing with people, with audiences, the abstraction is potentially misleading. When we feel an emotion strongly – with our pulses beating faster in fear, our faces flushing with anger, our hair bristling with fright – our senses and minds are normally involved in various degrees. In other words when we come to consider the ultimate effect of tragedy we must not confine our attention to one part of the traditional triad, mind, senses and emotions. We must approach it holistically and psychosomatically, in the same way as the Greeks generally approached questions of the human personality before philosophers spread the doctrine that the mind and the body were best considered as separable entities. As we have seen, the early ambiguities in words like *psuchē* and *phrēn* reflect the older holistic attitude.

The third possible wrong impression is a product of the second. In considering the ultimate effect of tragedy on *people* (and not on abstractions like minds, senses and emotions) is it sufficient to reckon only with the traditional triad? Not if we agree with so well qualified an authority on poetic drama as T. S. Eliot. In his essay entitled *Poetry and Drama* he observes:

> The chief effect of style and rhythm in dramatic speech, whether it be in prose or in verse, should be unconscious. . . . Of course when we have both seen a play several times and read it between performances, we begin to analyse the means by which the author has produced his effects. But in the immediate impact of the scene we are unconscious of the medium of its expression. . . .
>
> It seems to me that beyond the nameable and classifiable emotions of our conscious life when directed towards action – the part of life which prose drama is wholly adequate to express – there is a fringe of indefinite extent, of feeling which we can only detect, so to speak, out of the corner of the eye and can never completely focus; of feeling of which we are only aware in a kind of temporary detachment from action. . . . This peculiar range of sensibility can be expressed by dramatic poetry, at its moments of greatest intensity. At such moments we touch the border of those feelings which only music can express.

He goes further in affirming the importance of the non-rational effect of poetry in 'The Use of Poetry and the Use of Criticism':

> The chief use of the meaning of a poem in the ordinary sense may be (for here again I am speaking of some kinds of poetry – not all) to satisfy a habit of the reader, to keep

his mind diverted while the poem does its work upon him: much as the imaginary burglar is always provided with a bit of nice meat for the house-dog.

Eliot prudently avoided trying to give a precise definition either of how the poem performs its work, or of what the feeling is which we can only detect out of the corner of our eye – just as Yeats does not try to define how poetry works what he calls 'enchantment'. It would need someone highly skilled both in psychology and in the nature and function of poetry to succeed in that, and the present writer has no competence even to attempt it. But it may be remarked that when Eliot asserts that only music can express certain feelings the assertion does not apply to much of Greek dramatic poetry with its choral music and with the sub-music of its spoken parts. As we have seen, the use of the holistic term *mousikḗ* for both poetry and music embodied a belief that both were identical in essentials.

Secondly, even if the Greeks had no clear conception of the unconscious part of the *psuchḗ*, their ignorance did not preclude their poetry from unconsciously containing expressions of the unconscious. Some possible examples of this have already been noticed, and many others have been suggested by commentators skilled in psychology. Besides, the familiar phenomena of dreams and poetic inspiration and prophecy offered evidence to the ancient Greeks that there was a source of feelings, images and thoughts, beyond the reach of the conscious mind. The fact that they generally attributed these to divine interventions is immaterial so far as their practical effect is concerned. Similarly the language of myth offers sumbolisms that psychologists have accepted as expressions of the unconscious.

Finally, can we in the light of these considerations reach any valid conclusions about the nature of Greek tragedy's total effect on the whole *psuchḗ*? This is different from asking that unanswered and perhaps unanswerable question of what exactly Aristotle meant by his doctrine of the catharsis. In it he was dealing with the emotions alone, a necessary limitation for the purpose of refuting Plato's condemnation of tragic emotionalism. What concerns the present study is the more general principle of *psuchagōgía*, which, as we have seen in chapter 1, was the dominant criterion of effective discourse poetry before and after Plato and Aristotle.

Plato, who offers so many valuable insights into the nature of poetry, describes in his *Laws* 790C–791B a process that has often been cited in connection with the therapeutic power of music. The subject under discussion is the treatment of restless children. In the dialogue the Athenian Stranger notes the paradox that when mothers want to lull restless children to sleep they do not offer them quietness, but, on the contrary, movement. They take them in their arms and keep rocking them. Nor do they offer them silence. Instead they sing to them. In that way they restore the children to tranquillity of their *psuchē*, much as players on the pipe can calm people, and as victims of the Corybantic frenzy are treated by the combined movements of dance and song. The obvious objection to using these familiar phenomena in ancient Athens as analogies for the experience of the Athenian audiences at the tragic performances is that those audiences were adult and sane, not infantile and mad. But when Aristotle in his extended discussion of the ethical and emotional power of music in *Politics* 1341b 32ff. follows Plato in citing Corybantism, he does not limit the value of music to those who suffered from that distressing complaint (similar in its nature and treatment to the tarantism of southern Italy). He says that some degree of *páthos* – of *éleos* and *phóbos*, for example – is present in everyone, and everyone to some extent can experience some 'catharsis and a lightening accompanied by pleasure' from hearing the right kind of music. (Plato, it will be remembered, admitted that 'even the best of us' are affected by the emotionalism of tragedy.) In simple terms, one did not need to be psychologically sick to have benefit from the right kind of music. Besides, though Plato and Aristotle do not mention this in the passages just cited, the tragedies were a development from a cult similar to that of the Corybantes, the orgiastic cult of Dionysos with its compelling music and dancing. We should remember, too, that the Athenians came to the Dionysian Festival when spring had reawakened passions and desires after the rigours of the winter.

As to Plato's first example of treating movement homo-eopathically by movement, any analogy between an infant being rocked and sung to rest by its mother and a sophisticated audience seems quite absurd at first sight. But second consider-ations, as Pindar affirms, are sometimes best. The problem in dealing with disturbed infants is that they are *in-fantes* 'non-speakers'. They cannot tell you what is wrong with them. They can only utter animal cries, like Hecuba and Oedipus and Cassandra in their moments of supreme agony. The uncon-scious element in our natures (I avoid calling it 'the uncon-scious mind', as that begs a big question) is an infant in the same sense. It cannot tell what is wrong or what it wants. It can only 'mutter in darkness' to use the words of the anxious chorus in *Agamemnon* 1030. And are there any human beings, past or present, who at some times in their lives have not felt, under stress of inexpressible troubles, like an infant crying in the night?

If we accept these analogies, we may perhaps understand the *psuchagōgía* of tragedy at its best as being a process something like this: the complex, co-ordinated movements of rhythm, voice-melody, instrumental music, dance, gesture, imagery and 'story' drew the *psuchaí* of the audience into its *molpḗ*, just as the *molpḗ* of Dionysos in Euripides' *Bacchai* drew all the Thebans, except Pentheus and his minions, into the sacred orgies. As the drama gathered momentum towards its climax, like a flooding river it drew their jangling thoughts, feelings and sensations into its controlled current and harmonized them in its flow. Once the climax was passed and the drama's movement gradually grew quiet, the audience were quietened with it – not in 'calm of mind all passion spent' as Milton described it at the end of his *Samson Agonistes*, but in harmony of the whole *psuchḗ*, all *tarachḗ* removed . . . for a while.

Abbreviations

AJP	*American Journal of Philology*
CP	*Classical Philology*
CQ	*Classical Quarterly*
CR	*Classical Review*
CW	*Classical Weekly*
H	*Hermes*
HSCP	*Harvard Studies in Classical Philology*
Ph	*Philologus*
Phoen.	*Phoenix*
SO	*Symbolae Osloenses*
S–S¹	*Geschichte der Griechischen Literatur* by W. Schmid and O. Stählin, Part 1 and 2 (Munich 1934)
S-S²	the same, Part 1 vol. 3 (Munich 1940)
TAPA	*Transactions of the American Philological Association*

References

For bibliographies of relevant works earlier than 1934 on Aeschylus and Sophocles see S–S¹ and for those earlier than 1940 on Euripides see S–S². Where these and other general studies are cited, their indexes should be consulted.

CHAPTER 1

For general discussion of emotionalism in Greek tragedy I am indebted to: Burkert; Howald; Lesky; Otis; Pohlenz; Romilly (especially); Schadewaldt; Shisler (1945); Snell; Taplin (1978); Vickers. On *psuchagōgía*: Romilly (1975); Segal (1962); Solmsen. On the paradoxical pleasure of grief: Pucci. On audiences' reactions: Bain; Oranje; Pickard-Cambridge; Taplin (1978); Vickers. On *enthousiasmós*: Dodds (1951); W. D. Smith in *TAPA* 96 (1965) 403–26. On the journal quoted: 'The Manuscripts of Lord Charlemont's Eastern Travels', *Proceedings of the Royal Irish Academy* 80 C3 (1980) 13–91. On Nietzsche and Greek tragedy: W. Arrowsmith, *Arion* 2 (1963) *passim*; M. S. Silk and J. P. Stern, *Nietzsche on Tragedy* (Cambridge 1981).

CHAPTER 2

On conditions of performances: P. Arnott, *Greek Scenic Conventions in the Fifth Century BC* (Oxford 1962); Pickard-Cambridge; Spitzbarth; Walcot. On the effects of wine: Flashar p. 45. On audiences' pre-knowledge of plots: S–S¹ (153 n.4) in contrast with Taplin (1977) 27–8.

CHAPTER 3

On ancient opinions on the nature of the emotions and the *psuchē*: W. W. Fortenbaugh, *Aristotle on Emotion* (London 1975); W. Lyons, *Emotion* (Cambridge 1980); D. B. Claus *Toward the Soul* (New Haven 1981). On the medical approach: Flashar. On pity and grief: Aulitzky; Burkert; Doll; Erffa; Flashar; A. Klocker, Wortgeschichte von éleos und oîktos in der gr. Dichtung und Philosophie von Homer bis Aristoteles (diss. Innsbruck 1953); Lucas (1962); G. H. Macurdy, *The Quality of Mercy* (New Haven 1940);

References

Pohlenz (1956); Pucci; Romilly (1961); Schadewaldt (1955); S–S[1,2] (indexes at *Mitleid*); E. B. Stevens in *AJP* 65 (1944) 1–25; Winnington-Ingram. On *philanthrōpía*: S. Tromp de Ruiter, 'De vocis quae est *philanthrōpía* significatione atque usu', *Mnemosyne* 59 (1932) 271–306; Snell (1953). On fear: Coleman; T. Feldmann, 'Gorgo and the Origins of Fear', *Arion* 4 (1965) 484–94; Flashar; Lucas (1968); Pohlenz (1956); Schadewaldt (1955); S–S[1,2] (*Furcht*). Anger and hate: R. Camerer, *Zorn und Groll in der sophokleische Tragoedie* (Leipzig 1936); Knox; Romilly (1977 *bis*); T. Rosenmeyer in *Phoen.* 6 (1952) 93–112; Stanford (1981). On *phthónos* and *némesis*: S–S[1,2] (*Neid*). On shame: Barrett; Dodds (1925); D. Kovacs in *AJP* 101 (1980) 287–303; S–S[1,2] (*Aidos*); Stanford (1981). On *érōs*: J. Boardman and E. La Rocca, *Eros in Greece* (London 1978); S–S[1,2] (*Eros*). On *póthos*: V. Ehrenberg in *JHS* 67 (1947) 65–7 and in *Alexander and the Greeks* (Oxford 1938) 56–61; Segal (1962). On *philopatría*: H. R. Butts, 'The Glorification of Athens in Greek Drama', *Iowa Studies in Classical Philology* 11 (1947); S–S[1,2] (*Heimatliebe, Vaterland*); Walcot. On *enthousiasmós*: see on chapter 1. On joy: Shisler (1942). On special treatment of emotions by the three tragedians: (Aeschylus) Coleman; Doll; Fraenkel; Lesky; Romilly (1958, 1961, 1977); Snell (1928); S–S[1] (*Affekte, Gefühl, Leidenschaft, Pathos*); Thalmann; (Sophocles) Jaene; Knox; Long; Romilly (1961); Schadewaldt (1947); S–S[1] (ibid.); Webster (1936); (Euripides) Bond; Jaene; Lesky; Oranje; Pucci; Romilly (1961); S–S[2] (ibid.); Waardenburg. On popular attitudes to various emotions in everyday life: Dover. On the various emotions (besides grief) in tragic *Kommoí*: F. M. Cornford in *CR* 27 (1913) 41–5.

CHAPTER 4

On music in Greek tragedy: R. Browning, 'A Byzantine Treatise on Tragedy', *Geras: Studies Presented to George Thomson*, ed. L. Varcl and R. F. Willetts (Prague 1963) 67–81; H. R. Fairclough, 'The Connection between Music and Poetry in Early Greek Literature', *Studies in Honour of Basil Gildersleeve* (Baltimore 1902); A. J. Festugière, 'L'âme et la musique d'après Aristide Quintilien,' *TAPA* 85 (1954) 55–78; Kranz; E.A. Lippmann, *Musical Thought in Ancient Greece* (New York 1964); M. Pintacuda, *La musica nella tragedia graeca* (Cefalù 1978); R. P. Winnington-Ingram, article on 'Music' in *The Oxford Classical Dictionary* (2nd edn, Oxford 1970) from which (p. 708) the quotation on melody is taken. On the modes: M. L. West, 'The Singing of Homer and the Modes of Greek Music', *JHS* 101 (1981) 113–29. On musical accompaniments to films: J. H. Limbacher (ed.), *Film Music from Violins to Video* (Metuchen, NJ, 1974). On interjections and exclamatory cries: H. Deubner, 'Ololyge und Verwandtes', *Abhandl. der Preuss. Akad.* Phil.-Hist. Classe 1941, 1; J. A. Haldane, 'Barbaric Cries' (Aeschylus, *Persians* 633–9)', *CQ* 22 (1972) 42–50; Kiefer; S–S[1,2] (*Interjektionen*); E. Schwyzer, *Gr. Grammatik* 2 (Berlin 1950). On ritual lamentation: M. Alexiou, *The Ritual Lament in Greek Tradition* (Cambridge 1974). On silences: Mastronarde; S–S[1,2] (*Schweigen*); Taplin (1972, 1978). On emotional outbursts: Bain, Zucker.

171

References

CHAPTER 5

On the survival of the oral tradition until the fifth century: E. A. Havelock, *Preface to Plato* (Cambridge, Mass. 1963) and *The Literate Revolution in Greece and its Consequences* (Princeton 1982). On aesthetic and emotional aspects of the Greek language: Stanford (1967) and in *GR* 28 (1981) 127–40 with further bibliography to date (but add R. B. Egan, *The Assonance of Athena and the Sound of the Salpinx: Eumenides* 566–71 in *CJ* 74 (1979) 203–12; and see S–S[1],[2] (*Alliteration, Klangfiguren*). On Yeats's views: V. C. Clinton-Baddely in *The London Magazine* 4 (1957) 47–53. On significant rhythm: Headlam and Thomson (2, 327–9, 332–4); Lloyd-Jones; Otis; G. Thomson, *Greek Lyric Metre* 2nd edn (Cambridge 1961). On metrical resolutions: Zucker.

CHAPTER 6

On emotive visual elements in general: Shisler (1945); Segal; Spitzbarth; Taplin (1978); Vickers. On *ópsis*: Lucas (1968); B. Marzullo in *Phoen* 124 (1980) 189–200; A. Stigen, 'On the Alleged Primacy of Sight . . . in Aristotle', *SO* 36 (1960) 15–44. On costume: S–S[2] (*Bettlerkostüm*); Taplin (1977, 1978). On colour-symbolism: Goheen (1955); Lebeck. On stage properties, objects and tokens: Taplin (1978). On facial expression: Taplin (1978), Vickers. On masks: Pickard-Cambridge; Webster (1970 and in *Classical Drama and its Influence* ed. M. J. Anderson, London 1965). On gestures: H. Ortkemper, 'Szenische Techniken bei Euripides: Untersuchungen zur Gebärdsprache im antiken Theater' (diss. Berlin 1969), Segal; Shisler; Spitzbarth; Taplin (1978). On the movements of Greek dancing: L. B. Lawler in *TAPA* 85 (1954) 148–58; Webster (1970). On 'the Fearsome Dance': L. B. Lawler in *AJP* 67 (1946) 67–70.

CHAPTER 7

On Greek rhetorical attitudes to emotionalism in general: G. Kennedy, *The Art of Persuasion in Greece* (Princeton 1963); Martin; Solmsen, Thesleff. On abstract terms: Long; S–S[1],[2] (*Abstrakta*). On repetitions and refrains: Bond; Fraenkel; O. Hiltbrunner, 'Wiederholungs- und Motivtechnik bei Aischylos' (diss. Bern 1950); Kells; K. A. Kelly, 'Variable Repetition: Word Patterns in the Persae', *CJ* 74 (1979) 213–19; Kranz; H. E. Moritz in *CP* 74 (1979) 187–213; S–S[1],[2] (*Anaphora, Anadiplosis, Refrain, Wortverdopplung, Wiederholung*); Thesleff; Webster (1970). On isometric rhyming repetitions: J. Diggle in *CR* 18 (1968) 3–4. On aposiopesis and anacolouthon: Martin; Mastronarde; S–S[1] pp. 298, 490; S–S[2] p. 810, and at *Schweigen*. On asyndeton and hyperbaton: Bond; Fraenkel; Kells; Stanford (1981); Zucker. On antilabe: S–S[1],[2] (*Antilabe*). Aporetic questions: Bond (p. 386); S–S[1],[2] (*Frage*). Pleonasm and tautology: Bond; Fraenkel; S–S[1],[2] (*Tautologie, Pleonasmen*); Stanford (1981). Hyperbole: S–S[1],[2] (*Hyperbel*). Paronomasia:

172

References

S–S[1,2] (*Etymologien, Figura etymologica, Wortspiel*). Oxymoron: D. Fehling in *Hermes* 96 (168) 142–55; S–S[1,2] (*Oxymoron*). On ambiguity: Stanford (1972). On emotional *dé*: J. D. Denniston, *The Greek Particles*, 2nd edn (Oxford 1954) 214–15.

CHAPTER 8

On metaphors, similes and imagery: Barlow; Cameron; Dumortier; B. H. Fowler in *Classica et Mediaevalia* 28 (1967) 1–74; Goheen (1951); Long; Musurillo; Peradotto; Petrounias; Segal; Shisler (1942); Stanford (*Metaphor, Aeschylus*, and *Ajax*). Thalmann; Webster (1936). On spider and snake imagery: Devereux; W. Whallon in *TAPA* 89 (1958) 35–41. On lion imagery: B. M. W. Knox in *CP* 47 (1951) 271–5. On perverted imagery: Vickers; F. I. Zeitlin in *TAPA* 96 (1965) 463–508. On personification: Long; S–S[1,2] (*Personifikation*). On recurrent imagery: P. Biggs, in *CP* 61 (1966) 223–5; Goheen (1951); Musurillo; Peradotto; Stanford (*Aeschylus*); Thalmann. On irony: G. M. Kirkwood, *A Study of Sophoclean Drama* (Ithaca, NY 1958); S–S[1,2] (*Ironie*). On difficulties in the meaning of *páthos* in *Poetics*: Lucas; B. R. Rees in *GR* 19 (1972) 1–11. On plot and *peripéteia*: Lucas (1962 and 1968).

CHAPTER 9

On aspects of Aeschylus relevant to this chapter (besides the works cited in the text): Cameron; Romilly (1958, 1961, 1977); Snell (1928); S–S[1] pp. 222–37; Stanford (*Aeschylus*); Taplin (1977, 1978); Vickers.

Works cited

(For abbreviations see page 169)

Aulitzky, K., 'Apsines *perì eléou*', *Wiener Studien* 39 (1917) 26–49.
Bain, D., *Actors and Audience*, Oxford 1979.
Barlow, S. A., *The Imagery of Euripides*, London 1971.
Barrett, W. S., *Euripides: Hippolytos*, Oxford 1964.
Bond, G. W., *Euripides: Heracles*, Oxford 1981.
Burkert, W., *Zum altgriechischen Mitleidsbegriff*, Erlangen 1955.
Cameron, W. M., *Studies in the Seven against Thebes of Aeschylus*, The Hague 1971.
Coleman, W. Mc., 'The Role of Fear in the Social Order of Aeschylus', diss. Tallahasse, 1973.
Denniston, J. D. and Page, D., *Aeschylus: Agamemnon*, Oxford 1957.
Devereux, G., *Dreams in Greek Tragedy*, Oxford 1976.
Dodds, E. R., 'The *aidós* of Phaedra and the Meaning of the *Hippolytos*', *CR* 37 (1925) 102–4.
Dodds, E. R., *The Greeks and the Irrational*, Cambridge 1951.
Doll, F., 'Das Mitleid in der Tragödie des Aischylos und Sophokles', diss. Freiburg 1945.
Dover, K. J., *Greek Popular Morality in the Time of Plato and Aristotle*, Oxford 1974.
Dumortier, J., *Les images dans la poésie d'Eschyle*, Paris 1935.
Erffa, C. E. von, 'Aidós und verwandte Begriffe . . .', *Ph.* Supplementband 30 (1937) 2.
Flashar, H., 'Die medizinischen Grundlagen der Lehre von der Wirkung der Dichtung in der gr. Poetik', *H* 84 (1956) 12–48.
Fraenkel, E., *Aeschylus: Agamemnon*, 3 vols, Oxford 1950.
Goheen, R. F., *The Imagery of Sophocles' Antigone*, Princeton 1951.
Goheen, R. F., 'Aspects of Dramatic Symbolism: Three Studies in the Oresteia', *AJP* 76 (1955) 113–37.
Groeneboom, P., *Aeschylus' Agamemnon*, Groningen 1944.
Headlam, W. G., and Thomson, G., *The Oresteia of Aeschylus*, 2 vols, Cambridge 1938.
Henderson, J., *The Maculate Muse*, New Haven 1975.
Howald, E., *Die gr. Tragödie*, Munich 1930.
Jaene, H. E., 'Die Funktion des Pathetischen im Aufbau sophokleischer und euripideischer Tragödien', diss. Kiel 1929.
Jones, J., *Aristotle and Greek Tragedy*, London 1962.

Works cited

Kells, J. H., *Sophocles: Electra*, Cambridge 1973.

Kiefer, K., 'Körperlicher Schmerz und Tod auf der attischer Bühne', diss. Heidelberg 1909.

Knox, B. M. W., *The Heroic Temper: Studies in Sophoclean Tragedy*, Berkeley 1964.

Kranz, W., *Stasimon: Untersuchungen zu Form und Gehalt der gr. Tragödie*, Berlin 1933.

Lebeck, A., *The 'Oresteia'. A Study in Language and Structure*, Washington, DC 1971.

Lesky, A., 'Psychologie bei Euripides', *Entretiens de la Fondation Hardt* 6 (1958) 123–68.

Lesky, A., 'Sophokles und das Humane', *Gesammelte Schriften*, ed. W. Kraus, Bern 1966, pp. 275–80.

Lesky, A., 'Zur Problematik des Psychologischen in der Tragödie des Euripides', ibid., pp. 247–63.

Lloyd-Jones, H., *Agamemnon by Aeschylus*, Englewood Cliffs, N J 1970.

Long, A. A., *Language and Thought in Sophocles: a Study of Abstract Nouns and Poetic Technique*, London 1968.

Lucas, D. W., 'Pity, Terror, and Peripeteia', *CQ* 12 (1962) 52–60.

Lucas, D. W., *Aristotle: Poetics*, Oxford 1968.

Martin, J., *Antike Rhetorik*, Munich 1974.

Mastronarde, D. J., *Continuity and Discontinuity: Some Conventions of Speech and Action on the Greek Tragic Stage*, Berkeley 1979.

Musurillo, H., *The Light and the Darkness: Studies in the Dramatic Poetry of Sophocles*, Leiden 1969.

Oranje, H., *De Bacchae von Euripides het stuk en de toeschouwers*, Amsterdam 1979.

Otis, Brooks, *Cosmos and Tragedy: an Essay on the Meaning of Aeschylus*, ed. C. Kopf, Chapel Hill 1981.

Peradotto, J. J., 'Some Patterns of Nature Imagery in the Oresteia', *AJP* 85 (1964) 378–93.

Petrourias, E., *Funktion und Thematik der Bilder bei Aischylos*, Göttingen 1976.

Pickard-Cambridge, Sir Arthur, *The Dramatic Festivals of Athens*, 2nd edn revised by J. Gould and D. M. Lewis, Oxford 1968.

Pohlenz, M., *Die gr. Tragödie*, Göttingen 1954.

Pohlenz, M., 'Furcht und Mitleid! Ein Nachwort', *H* 84 (1956) 49–74.

Pucci, P., *The Violence of Pity in Euripides' Medea*, Ithaca, N Y 1980.

Romilly, J. de, *La crainte et l'angoisse dans la theâtre d'Eschyle*, Paris 1958.

Romilly, J. de, *L'evolution du pathétique d'Eschyle à Euripide*, Paris 1961.

Romilly, J. de, *Magic and Rhetoric in Ancient Greece*, Cambridge, Mass. 1975.

Romilly, J. de, 'La haine dans l'*Orestie*', *Dioniso* 48 (1977) 33–53.

Romilly, J. de, 'La haine et l'inimitié dans Homère', *Ancient and Modern Essays in Honor of Gerald F. Else*, ed. J. H. D'Arms and J. W. Eadie, Ann Arbor 1977, pp. 1–10.

Rose, H. J., *A Commentary on the Surviving Plays of Aeschylus*, 2 vols, Amsterdam 1957–8.

Works cited

Schadewaldt, W., *Sophokles und das Leid*, Potsdam 1947.

Schadewaldt, W., 'Furcht und Mitleid', *H* 83 (1955) 129–71.

Segal, C. P., 'Gorgias and the Psychology of the Logos', *HSCP* 66 (1962) 99–155.

Segal, C., 'Visual Symbolism and Visual Effects in Sophocles', *Classical Weekly* 74 (1980) 125–42.

Shisler, F. L., 'The Technique of the Portrayal of Joy in Greek Tragedy', *TAPA* 73 (1942) 277–92.

Shisler, F. L., 'The Use of Stage Business to Portray Emotion in Greek Tragedy', *AJP* 66 (1945) 377–97.

Snell, B., 'Aischylos und das Handeln im Drama', *Ph* Supplementband 20 (1928) 1.

Snell, B., *The Discovery of the Mind*, translated by T. Rosenmeyer, Oxford 1953.

Solmsen, F., 'Aristotle and Cicero on the Orator's Playing upon the Emotions', *CP* 33 (1938) 390–404.

Spitzbarth, A., *Untersuchungen zur Spieltechnik der gr. Tragödie*, Zurich 1946.

Stanford, W. B., *Greek Metaphor*, corrected reprint, New York 1972.

Stanford, W. B., *Ambiguity in Greek Literature*, corrected reprint, New York 1972.

Stanford, W. B., *Aeschylus in His Style*, corrected reprint, New York 1972.

Stanford, W. B., *Sophocles: Ajax*, corrected reprint, Bristol 1981.

Stanford, W. B., *The Sound of Greek*, Berkeley 1967.

Taplin, O., 'Aeschylean Silences and Silences in Aeschylus', *HSCP* 76 (1972) 57–97.

Taplin, O., *The Stagecraft of Aeschylus*, Oxford 1977.

Taplin, O., *Greek Tragedy in Action*, Oxford 1978.

Thalmann, W. G., *Dramatic Art in Aeschylus's Seven Against Thebes*, New Haven 1978.

Thesleff, H., *Studies on Intensification in Early and Classical Greek*, Helsingfors 1954.

Thomson, G., *Greek Lyric Metre*, 2nd edn, Cambridge 1961.

Thomson, G., *see* Headlam.

Vickers, B., *Towards Greek Tragedy*, London 1973.

Walcot, P., *Greek Drama in its Theatrical and Social Setting*, Cambridge 1976.

Webster, T. B. L., *An Introduction to Sophocles*, Oxford 1936.

Webster, T. B. L., 'Some Psychological Terms in Greek Tragedy', *JHS* 77 (1959) 149–54.

Webster, T. B. L., *The Greek Chorus*, London 1970.

Winnington-Ingram, R. P., *Sophocles: an Interpretation*, Cambridge 1980.

Zucker, F., 'Formen Gesteigert Rede in Sprechversen der gr. Tragödie', *Indogermanische Forschungen* 62 (1956) 62–77.

Index 1
Proper names and dramatic characters

Index 4 should also be consulted for the tragedians

Index 2
General topics
See also Index 3

Index two

Index 3
Selective list of Greek terms

Index 4
Passages quoted from Greek tragedy

For other authors see Index 1

Index four